A IS FOR ALEX

A IS FOR ALEX

A Bereaved Mother's Promise to her Beloved Son

Lesley Roberts

Cherish
EDITIONS

First published in Great Britain 2021 by Cherish Editions

Cherish Editions is a trading style of Shaw Callaghan Ltd & Shaw Callaghan 23 USA, INC.

The Foundation Centre

Navigation House, 48 Millgate, Newark

Nottinghamshire NG24 4TS UK

www.cherisheditions.com

British Library Cataloguing in Publication Data

A CIP catalogue record for this book is available upon request from the British Library

ISBN: 978-1-913615-47-5

This book is also available in the following eBook formats:

ePUB: 978-1-913615-48-2

Lesley Roberts has asserted her right under the Copyright, Design and Patents Act 1988 to be identified as the author of this work

Cover design by Fusion Graphic Design

Typeset by Lapiz Digital Services

Paper from responsible sources

For Alex,
I wish I had known.

Love Always and Forever,
Mum
xxx

"I loved the Boy with the utmost love of which my soul is capable, and he is taken from me — yet in the agony of my spirit in surrendering such a treasure, I feel a thousand times richer than if I had never possessed it."

William Wordsworth

FOREWORD

The agony of losing a child of any age is unparalleled. There is no
age or point in time that makes it any more bearable. It goes against
the natural order of life, and the pain is compounded by losing
a child to suicide. Suicide is the leading cause of death amongst
young males. According to a recent article published in Canada,
the number of people who die by suicide in that country each
year equates to a jumbo jet crashing and killing everyone on board
every single month of the year – truly shocking. Another horrifying
statistic is that there were 5,691 suicides in England and Wales
in 2019, and suicide is the leading cause of death among men in
the 20-to-50 age group in the UK. I did not know these alarming
statistics and, as my son had no history of mental health problems,
his suicide was a complete and devastating shock. Nobody close
to him had any idea that he was suffering and yet our tragedy was
already playing out in slow motion.

Suicide leaves heartbreak in its wake, and the stigma attached to
such tragedies adds to the isolating agony for the bereaved families
left behind. There is one simple thing we can do to reduce the stigma
around suicide: to acknowledge the power of language and stop using
the word "commit" to prefix suicide. Commit has the connotation of
criminality, and suicide is not a crime. It is the act of a person in the
most desperately dark and often lonely place.

In Victorian times, suicide was indeed considered a crime, and
in the United Kingdom, it was not until The Crimes Act 1958 that
suicide ceased officially to be an illegal act. Although the criminal
associations with suicide have disappeared, the phrase "committed
suicide" is often still used, and it is time we updated our terminology.

My son did not "commit" suicide. He was a law-abiding, gentle, loving son and brother who tragically "died by suicide". Alex had lost hope for a happy future for himself, and he wanted to free himself from his pain. This is a tragedy, not a crime.

Language matters. Given the magnitude of shame and stigma surrounding suicide and its impact on the process of grief, it helps to refer to the method of death less judgmentally as "death by suicide", "took their own life" or "suicide death". Perhaps some reading this may learn from Alex's story and alter their use of language in his memory. Prior to Alex's death, I did not know that those bereaved by suicide have a preference for the language used to describe their loved one's death. Sadly, I do now, and I have learnt this is a cause for additional difficulty for many survivors. It can be wounding to bereaved families when a person who died this way is referred to as "a suicide". We would never say someone was "a heart attack". Alex died as a result of suicide, but please do not refer to him as "a suicide". He was so much more than that. Choice of words matter in this sensitive and heart-breaking arena, and the power of language is important.

Furthermore, research shows that there is far less obvious sympathy and support for the families left behind following a death by suicide, and sadly I can attest to this. Having heard from other bereaved parents, it seems that the death of a child or young adult can and does often result in former relationships becoming strained or disappearing altogether.

It is a common narrative that suicide is a selfish act, and whilst I am living proof of the heartbreak my son's death has caused me, I have not for one second considered his action selfish. Alex was the strongest and most courageous person I have known. When Alex lost all hope, I believe he lost perspective. I know that my son did consider the impact of his death on his family, friends and colleagues, and he acknowledged this in his last, loving emails. The mind of a suicidal person is such a dark place that they believe their loved ones will be spared the burden of their suffering if they are no longer around. If only they knew how wrong they were…

Sadly, I did not see the signs that my beloved son was suffering, and when I came close, I accepted his false reassurances. Why couldn't I stop Alex from killing himself? In retrospect, the light in his eyes had dimmed, but he hid it so well from everyone. I truly believe that as a society, if we are to reduce the number of young men taking their own lives, we have to create an environment that encourages men to talk more about their problems, and, as in my son's case, most especially if they are sexual and of a personal nature. I bitterly regret that I did not consider broaching any dialogue with my sons about whether they had any issues with their genitals. If I had had daughters rather than sons, I am certain that the subjects of menstruation and sexual health would have been open topics of discussion, but, sadly, it never crossed my mind to ask my older sons if they had any sexual health problems. Tragically, Alex was suffering from phimosis, a painful condition that I had never even heard of until the torturous night of his death. I have since discovered that most of Alex's friends, all in their 20s, would also *not* have discussed with their mums any difficulty in their sexual health or pain in this personal part of their bodies. Perhaps they are just being kind in saying that to me, and if they are, thank you. If I had been more aware of men's sexual health, then I would have opened a conversation in which my sons could discuss their sexual concerns with me instead of just assuming they would if the need arose. I had a close and loving relationship with Alex. I therefore assumed that he felt comfortable discussing anything with me and yet, tragically, I had no idea that he was keeping from me his innermost private pain. I did not understand until it was too late that I must have failed to address this gap in my parenting and will probably never fully know why Alex did not share his suffering with me.

This book is also about the potential harm caused by circumcision. I am not medically trained so I can not offer any medical advice. I understand that circumcision is not wrong for all, yet I now believe it should be a last medical resort. It was disastrous for my son and many, many others, some of whom have contacted me to say how much the publicity surrounding Alex's tragic death has helped them talk about their own issues. I was humbled to be asked to become an ambassador for the charity 15 Square, so named as it is a reference to the upper amount of tissue that is typically removed during an adult circumcision. The charity was formed over 25 years ago to help men who have been damaged physically or psychologically – or often both – by circumcision. I have discovered through my work with the charity that medical conditions such as phimosis can be treated non-invasively. In Alex's memory, I hope other young men can be better informed about alternative, non-surgical and less invasive treatments, and the potential adverse consequences of circumcision. This is not helped by men not wanting to share the pain and embarrassment they face when their circumcision procedures go wrong. And they do. Not always, of course, but as I have come to learn since my son's death, too frequently to ignore.

I am now convinced that there is a link between circumcision and suicide, as I have learnt of other young men who have ended their lives because of the damage caused by their operations. I hope that doctors and urologists become more familiar with statistics of the devastating problems, both physical and mental, that can result from this procedure. There needs to be more research on the risks involved so people can make more informed choices based on adequate data.

ABOUT THE AUTHOR

My name is Lesley Roberts, and I am heartbroken to have become a member of the club no parent on earth wishes to join – that of a bereaved mum of a much-loved child who died by suicide. My darling son Alex took his own life on 24 November 2017, aged 23 years, 4 months and 10 days. At the time of completing my book, Alex left us 3 years and 6 months ago.

I write this book as a bereaved mother, and it is not my intention to either portray myself as a victim or Alex as a saint. He was brave, showed great dignity and tried to spare those he loved from his pain. I loved him with all my heart. The powerful words Alex left behind and shared in this book reflect his innate generosity in wanting to leave this world helping others. His description of his suffering has, and I am sure will, continue to provide support to the many other men damaged by circumcision. I am humbled that my son's articulate words have been acknowledged by some medical practitioners around the world to be both eloquent and insightful, so, perhaps after all, I can be forgiven for saying that Alex is my hero.

I don't want to be the mum of a dead son. Alex was an intelligent, witty, fun, kind, reserved, self-effacing, sensitive, hard-working, outdoorsy, quirky and gorgeous human being. I don't want to be talking publicly about things like foreskin, circumcision, coffins, funerals and ashes, but this is my new normal, my reality following Alex's circumcision at the age of 21 and related suicide two years later. The language I know has no words to adequately describe the pain, the horror, the never-ending yearning for my cherished son. Tragically, there were many parents before, and there will be many after me who will also lose their much-loved child to suicide, and more young lives will be cut short. This is the book I needed when no one around me could help, when no one understood the depth of the agony in my soul. I have felt so alone in my grief during the darkest days since Alex's suicide. I struggled to comprehend the physical pain deep inside of me that was impossible to describe. This book is for grieving parents because only they can truly understand such depths of hell. I hope that this book leads you gently toward strength when you are weak and hope when you are broken. I have found the will to continue my grief journey from Alex's brothers Tom and James, together with my husband Steve, but most especially from Alex, who I know is constantly beside me, spurring me on.

Why am I writing this book, a story so painful that to revisit each moment of my precious boy's life and death is to stab a knife into my own heart with every word?

Firstly, and above all else, is that I simply have to honour Alex's last request of me: to publicize his suffering in the hope of helping others. This is the last thing I can ever do for my darling boy and, as

I have discovered, to do so in my own words is infinitely preferable than reading inaccuracies elsewhere. It is a source of comfort to me that since Alex's story was first covered on BBC News Online, and subsequently via other media, men from all over the world have contacted me and the charity 15 Square to express how they relate to Alex's words and how this has helped them to cope with their suffering. Alex's story has had a powerful impact and is making a difference.

Secondly, writing is my therapy and has been my survival from those earliest days following the news of Alex's death. I was almost mute from the shock and grief and found it to be my only release from the darkness and pain engulfing me. Right from the start of my journey through my new hell, I have put my emotions into my writing, and those words have evolved into this book. Talking publicly is empowering and massively helps me adjust while I come to terms with the unthinkable that has landed like a bomb on my doorstep.

Thirdly, this book is my dedication to the son I waited several years for and whom I loved with all my heart. Alex was and always will be my eldest son, my kindred spirit. He was a part of my soul, and that part will always be missing. Alex was wise beyond his years, and I am only now, more than three years after his death, able to fully understand what his last words were telling me. Previously, I was too lost in my grief to appreciate his desire for me to live "a meaningful life". I get it now, Alex: this book, the talks and interviews I do in your memory have given my life meaning and, in so doing, have created your legacy. For any children born to Alex's brothers Tom and James, I hope that my book will be a way in which their wonderful Uncle Alex is not forgotten.

Fourthly, and most importantly, if I can help save the life of one other young adult considering suicide, or spare any other parent from experiencing the hell of choosing a coffin for their beloved child, then I will have achieved something. Suicide has historically been a taboo subject talked about in hushed tones or swept under the carpet. The stigma and lack of understanding surrounding men's sexual health must have contributed to Alex choosing not to share his pain. He must have felt so alone, and this was not helped by my own lack of knowledge in spotting the signs of his subtle withdrawal. As a society, we need to be better at talking about suicide. There is no cushioning against the pain that consumes you when it happens to someone you love.

Finally, I would also like this book to offer hope to any desperate parents in the earlier stages of their grief who have lost a cherished child in this horrific way. I do not pretend to be an authority on suicide, but, sadly, I now know more than I wish I did. My book will hopefully serve as a helpful tool for those who know the bereaved family of a child who dies a sudden death. It may even facilitate reflection on the part of those close to me and my family who could – who should – have stepped up. Perhaps when another family loses a much-loved child to suicide, as tragically there will be others, those who can provide compassion and kindness might take something away from this book and spare another family some of the additional pain that mine has had to endure.

I never knew that I was statistically more likely to lose my son by suicide than in any other way. I question why I did not know this. To any other parent thrown into this disorientating abyss of grief and pain and doubting whether they can survive, as I have on many occasions, I want to offer you hope that you can survive the indescribable loss. You will emerge as a different version of your previous self, as you can never return to who you once were. I hope that my book can be a point of reference, a friend to any other bereaved parent navigating their way through their loss. After a child's death, we parents embark on a sad, lonely and never-ending journey that can be very alienating. There are no right or wrong ways to deal with this grief. The futures we imagined for our children are no longer possibile. All we can do is take small steps forward and accept there will be steps backward. I wish I could save others from this excruciating, unbearable pain, but whoever and wherever in the world you are, if you find yourself faced with the same tragedy, know that you are not alone. Breathe, take it one second at a time, live to say your child's name, share their memories, and know that your cherished child is with you and that you will hopefully be reunited one day. Be kind to yourself.

"We often wait for kindness…
but being kind to yourself can start now."
Charlie Mackesy, The Boy, the Mole, the Fox and the Horse

I do not profess to have yet reached a place where memories of my beloved son bring me light instead of profound sadness and unbearable grief, but I have found a painful, quiet place of peace in acceptance that however much I rail against it, my darling Alex is not coming back. The chronic, persistent pain he endured took him away from me forever on this earth. To reach that acceptance – and it is still ongoing – is an important step in my grief journey. I want what I cannot have: my boy back.

Perhaps this book might encourage parents who have a more sensitive, reserved child to not only trust their instincts, but to act upon them if they feel that something is not right. In my experience learnt so tragically, if you think something might be wrong, it probably is. If I had acted upon my deepest fears, I would not have waited a week following my last telephone conversation with Alex and would have gone to him on the very next available flight. Is it possible that my precious and adored son would still be here? It is too late for me to ever know. Our last conversation was chatty and loving as usual, yet I had a sense of unease that I still cannot articulate. I can best describe it as an anxiety in my subconscious mind. I wish I had been equipped to interpret the signs and language used by someone about to take their own life. Would I then have discovered if anything was wrong, or was I guilty of fussing and being overly anxious about nothing, as Alex had stated? I never considered that it would be too late a week later. If only I had known that experts in the subject of suicide say that asking direct questions will not encourage somebody already planning suicide to complete it. Asking questions like, "Are you thinking about hurting yourself?" or "Are you thinking about dying?" will not make it more likely to happen. Skirting around the issue won't help.

It is important to me to tell my story in my own words. My writing is the unvarnished truth, and if it evokes discomfort in some who read it, so be it. I have no doubt that Alex would have encouraged me to tell not only his story, as he asked of me in his last email, but also the parts of this tragedy that have been my experience.

In sharing Alex's story, I am reminded of a book, *Schindler's Ark* by Thomas Keneally, and the ensuing brilliant film, *Schindler's List*. When Schindler is chastising himself for not saving more of his workers, his accountant Itzhak Stern consoles him by quoting the Jewish Talmud: "He who saves one life, saves the world entire." If my darling Alex's story can help save one life, he won't have died in vain.

The horrific news of Alex's death did not reach me until Saturday, 25th November. Life before then seems like a faraway dream now, someone else's life, a happy life with my second husband Steve and my three lovely sons, Alex, Tom and James. It all came to a tragic, stomach-churning, horrific end with a knock at the door at 7pm on that dark evening in Cheshire. I was about to learn that my beloved first-born son had died approximately nine hours earlier…

CONTENTS

Chapter 1   Dreams Can Come True   1

Chapter 2   Growing Up In Cheshire, UK   7

Chapter 3   Letting Go   19

Chapter 4   When Time Stopped   27

Chapter 5   Returning to Canada   37

Chapter 6   Letting Go Forever   51

Chapter 7   Alex's Legacy   67

Chapter 8   The Agony of Suicide   81

Chapter 9   Living Without Alex   97

Chapter 10 What to Say (and Not to Say) to
            a Grieving Parent   109

Chapter 11 Meaning and Hope   117

Chapter 12 My Letter to Alex   129

"Somewhere over the rainbow,
skies are blue,
and the dreams that you dare to dream
really do come true."

The Wizard of Oz

CHAPTER 1

DREAMS CAN COME TRUE

All babies are special to their parents, but as this is my book, I feel entitled to say that Alex was especially so. My gorgeous son Alexander James was born on 14 July 1994, one week after my 30th birthday and following fertility treatment that itself had followed an ectopic pregnancy. The overwhelming love I felt for my son was indescribable when I first held my beautiful baby boy in my arms. I was reflecting recently that Alex's birth enabled me to become a member of the club I was desperate to join: motherhood. There were many times over the three years of fertility treatment when I feared I would always be on the outside looking in at other people's joy, yet here I was with my own baby. He could not have been more perfect.

The bond between a mum and her child starts in pregnancy and grows in infancy to a lifetime of unconditional love. I did not have an easy pregnancy, as I suffered with hyperemesis gravidarum, more commonly known as extreme morning sickness. It lasted the entire pregnancy, all day, every day, and lead to my hospitalization on several occasions. However, that was all forgotten the day he was born – truly the happiest day of my life.

Alex was a loving, adorable, placid and perceptive child who was full of curiosity. He was generous and kind when interacting with other children. I have an especially good memory, for which I am now truly grateful. If a child snatched a toy off Alex, he let them have it and would find another. He disliked confrontation and was easy-going. He seemed to have, from an early age, an innate understanding of the need for kindness and tolerance toward others. I often used to think that, in having to wait to become a mum, I was rewarded with the loveliest, kindest, gentlest and warm-hearted son. Alex was easy to please, loved home-cooked food, loved to sleep and smiled on waking. He happily played for hours with plastic farm animals, toy cars and trucks, and his treasured yellow-and-green plastic lawn mower. He would pretend to mow the lawn for hours from the age of only two, walking up and down the garden following his dad. Still, that couldn't compare to his absolute favourite toy of all: his plastic tool kit. I can still see him determinedly trying to drill and screw and bang nails into a piece of wood, busy mending things. Alex was always happiest outdoors, but most especially when fixing something.

I can be easily transported back to those happy days when Alex was very young and remember him saying his often-used first phrases. I can still hear the exact intonation in his voice. When Alex wanted to do something for himself, he would say determinedly, "Alex do it." When saying "All gone," he would stretch the word *alllllll* and would sound resigned in reluctant acceptance that he had finished his food, but he would always be smiling. Alex never had to be coaxed to eat, and his sunny disposition made being his mum such a joy – as I have said, an easy, adorable little boy. As if further proof were needed of my special bond with Alex, he and I were both left-handed and somehow, since losing my dear son, every small detail such as this has become significant and important to me.

Alex's early years were filled with such happy times spent largely with just me, as his father worked long hours. I would walk for miles along country lanes near to our home in North Wales with Alex snuggled in his pushchair, stopping occasionally to steal a kiss from my smiling boy or to point out a horse, cow, sheep or, more excitingly to Alex, a tractor, his favourite vehicle at that time. He would doze off and wake with the brightest of grins. I believe our close bond was formed during those years. As I write these words, I am reminded of several of his friends in Canada who told me after he died, "His smile could light up a room." How true. Who knew that my precious boy's enchanting smile from so many years ago would never change?

I remember as if it were yesterday a lovely holiday my then-husband, my parents and I took to Annecy, France, a few weeks after Alex's second birthday. I was just pregnant with Thomas and recall a visit to a bustling outdoor market on a particularly hot day. Alex was in his stroller, obscured by the large, attached sun canopy as we eased our way through the busy stalls, which had various goods displayed at all levels. Suddenly, I became aware of a green-and-yellow plastic wheelbarrow disappearing into the pushchair, having been spotted and grabbed by Alex! When I moved to look under the canopy, Alex was grinning proudly at his new acquisition on his knee. His smiling eyes made anything other than paying the stallholder for the new wheelbarrow impossible, and this remained a favourite toy for Alex for several years. I also recall Alex's first game of hide-and-seek around this time. He hadn't appreciated he needed to hide and instead crouched down in front of a tree within sight. We laughed – I can remember it as if it were yesterday, even the blue open-toe sandals he was wearing.

Alex seemed to understand how ill I was when fertility treatment worked for the second time, and I once again suffered an entire pregnancy with hyperemesis gravidarum. He displayed such a kind, loving and easy nature when I needed it most. My contented and placid toddler took it all in his stride and was delighted to welcome his gorgeous baby brother, Thomas, who was born when Alex was two years and nine months of age.

Physically, Alex was the healthiest of my three sons. He came into this world at 8lb, 11oz, and he rarely suffered any childhood illness, never broke a bone or needed hospital treatment, ate well, slept well and, thankfully, did not inherit my propensity for headaches and migraines, to which his brothers occasionally succumb. Alex hardly ever had a day off school – such was his robust health. The heart-breaking irony of this is not lost on me.

Life was perfect. I loved my little boys with all my heart. I remember clearly my parents arriving with Alex at the hospital following Thomas's birth. It was generally accepted that, in introducing a toddler to a new sibling, it can be helpful to present the older child with a gift from the new baby. When Alex arrived at the hospital to meet his baby brother, we gave him a new toy truck, but we need not have bothered: following hugs and kisses from me, he only had eyes for baby Thomas. Alex immediately asserted his role as the proud big brother and sat beside me on the bed asking to hold Thomas. He said, "He's my baby, Grandma, he's my baby," as if saying it twice would cement his position as the person who loved the baby the most. Alex's love and pride for Thomas is evident in the many photographs I now cherish from when the boys were very young.

From that very first moment of holding Thomas, his big brother loved him. Alex's gentle nature had no room for feelings of jealousy, and sibling rivalry was never present. I am, however, reminded of an incident many years later when the boys were teenagers. I had asked Thomas to go into Alex's bedroom, where Alex was at his desk, and bring me some printer paper. I had not expected him to waltz in and silently help himself. This must have irked Alex's usual easy-going nature because, in the next instant, Alex had pinned Thomas down and demanded to know what gave him the right to enter his bedroom and just take what he wanted. Did I say "gentle, caring, loving" …? Well, most of the time!

My beautiful boy Alexander James, aged 10 months, 1995

*"There is only one perfect child
in the world and every mother has it."*

Anonymous

CHAPTER 2

GROWING UP IN CHESHIRE, UK

Alex enjoyed attending the lovely local primary school, and he had many friends and regular play dates with his classmates. He was bright, excelled at English – especially spelling – and was particularly good at practical subjects, such as design technology. Outside of school, he could often be found on his bike and quickly became a proficient cyclist in and around the village where we lived. Alex and Thomas were close brothers and thrived at their school. They lived a sheltered and happy life until aged six and three, when a difficult time arose in our otherwise unexceptional lives.

My then-husband was involved in a terrible car accident when, alone in the car, he overtook and collided with an oncoming car that was also overtaking and whose driver, an elderly man, died at the scene of the accident. A traumatic court case followed and, ultimately, a ten-week prison term. The loss of a man's life was horrific, and the custodial sentence was a shock to everyone. When my husband returned, cracks in our marriage began to show, and, although we remained together for a further five years, we eventually divorced and both remarried.

Once Thomas joined Alex at primary school, I started a degree course in primary education and, upon completing this four years later, I knew immediately who I would like by my side for my graduation ceremony. Thomas was too young, so 11-year-old Alex, who had been so accommodating of my studies, was the obvious choice. I knew how proud he would be to accompany me to

Manchester for that day. I was equally proud of my wonderful eldest son by my side, and the photograph of Alex standing proudly beside me in my cap and gown is especially cherished.

Alex's favourite films during his primary school years were *Toy Story* and *Garfield* together with the *Wallace and Gromit* franchise. Perhaps, in time, I will be able to watch them again, but not yet. I spent many happy hours, especially on wet days, indoors snuggled up to a young Alex watching these films. I still think of him when I make one of his – and Garfield's – favourite dishes, lasagne. Years later, when Alex returned from Canada for a visit, I would cook it while he and his little brother James sat together and contentedly watched these childhood favourites again.

Alex left primary school the week of his 11th birthday and, as was then customary, the leaving year group performed an evening musical or play for their parents. Alex, being quite reserved, was not a natural performer, and he said little about the performance beforehand, being evasive about what his part would be. The musical was *Joseph and the Amazing Technicolor Dreamcoat*, and, as his year group opened the musical with their wonderful singing and acting, I was sad to see no sign of Alex. I was beginning to assume that he had a behind-the-scenes role when the music started for the arrival of Joseph, and, as the crowd in the scene parted, who should enter but Alex. He was amazing and slowly walked into the centre, swirling his fabulous coat around as his classmates sang "Any Dream Will Do". Other parents turned to look at me smiling, and I will never, ever forget my love and pride for my darling son taking centre stage. I think it took him great courage to do that, and it was brilliant casting by his teacher – thank you. I do not need to close my eyes to be transported back to that evening and am grateful that I have always had a good memory. Alex knew how proud I was that night, and I know how pleased he felt, despite his introverted character. He shone and was brilliant.

My first marriage ended when Alex was 11 and Thomas was 8, and the following year I married Steve, a lifelong friend since we had met in high school. I remember my happiness at walking down the aisle followed by Alex and Thomas in their smart navy-blue suits and purple ties, and my new husband's daughters, Emily and Alice, of similar age, looking beautiful in their cream-coloured bridesmaid dresses. It was a special day, and we took extra care to ensure that all our children felt included and loved throughout. We were so blessed, I know, that all our children always got on well, and this has never changed. It perhaps helped that Steve and I were friends from school days, and our children had always known each other. Of course, I am biased, but we had four wonderful children between us, soon to become five.

While we were anxious about introducing a new baby to them the following year, we need not have been. Alex, aged 13, greeted the news that we were expecting a new arrival with some concern and likely embarrassment, but as soon as he held James in his arms at the hospital, all his doubts melted away, and he was immediately smitten. All our children adored their new baby brother, but Alex especially so. He was particularly pleased that we chose the name James for our new son, as it was also Alex's middle name, which pleased him enormously and gave his position in his brother's life a slight edge over his siblings!

Around the time of James's birth and for a few years thereafter, I was a part-time primary school teacher specializing in French. Alex was especially helpful and loving at this time as James's birth was difficult and resulted in an emergency caesarean. Alex adored his baby brother and would hold out his arms to take James from me as I returned from work, having collected James from nursery school on the way home. Alex would happily take James for a bath, ably assisted by Thomas, but it was my eldest who took the lead, his position unassailable by virtue of three years seniority. I decided to leave teaching when Alex was 16 and approaching his GCSEs. Thomas was also at high school, and James was approaching school age. I felt the need to be there for my boys. It had become too difficult juggling the needs of their widely differing ages, with teaching and marking books late into the evening, as well as James spending long days at nursery school. Becoming a stay-at-home mum again, as I had been during Alex and Thomas's early years, was a better fit for the whole family.

James could do no wrong in Alex's eyes, and their close bond never changed. I know that being apart from James was difficult for Alex when he left home, and I remain certain that one of the reasons that Alex lived in pain for two years following his circumcision was his distress at the thought of leaving his little brother. He also must have known the sadness his death would inflict on James, who was only ten years old when Alex died.

Alex had limitless love and patience for his baby brother, just as he had all those years before when he was only a toddler and Thomas was born. I remember during Alex's teenage years when James was very young and, later, when James started school, there were times when I was preparing the evening meal and James needed occupying. I often silently delivered James to Alex's bedroom so he could give me a brief respite! No words were needed between Alex and me, just a look. He instantly knew I needed rescuing, and he was always happy to oblige. He would stop whatever he was doing, sit James on his knee and, within minutes, James was happy, often watching programmes from Alex's childhood such as *Bodger & Badger* and his particular favourite, *Brum*. Alex's endless love of being James's big brother shone brightly, and he was always happy to spend time with him.

I thought long and hard over whether to include the next few paragraphs in this book but, ultimately, I decided that, for this book to paint the whole of Alex's story, these events need to be included. For my own part, I have no desire to revisit such times. Suffice it to say, these painful events in Alex's life must have affected the young man he was to become, a young man who had known hurt, but who had come to terms with having no relationship with his dad in the last nine years of his life. In Alex's last email he described his strength and resilience at largely overcoming this loss.

My ex-husband did not invite Alex and Thomas to his wedding, and this caused them much pain. He told them that it was to be a small register office wedding with a couple of witnesses. Although I cannot be entirely sure of the reason for such lies, both of my sons felt at the time that their dad's new wife was not happy to have them around. They described sulks and slammed doors when they were in their home for their fortnightly visits, which, incidentally, tailed off by the time Alex was 14.

Months later, I was told by a mutual acquaintance that their ceremony had, in fact, been a big, white wedding at a large hotel with children in attendance, including the bride's young nephews. I felt sick upon hearing this, but knew that the boys had to be told, and that hearing it gently from me would be better than finding out from anyone else. How my ex-husband hoped to maintain his lie, I have no idea, as Thomas subsequently told me that there were photographs of the wedding in his father's house. As I have mentioned previously, I have an especially good memory, and I recall, as if it were an hour ago, my knotted stomach waiting to tell my lovely boys of their dad's wedding deceit because I knew that it would cause them pain. Both boys looked sad and shocked and went to their respective bedrooms to process the news. I told them how much they were loved and that, despite their dad making a bad decision, he loved them very much. The boys' relationship with their dad never recovered, and it became apparent to the boys over the following months that their presence was unwelcome in their dad's new life.

Alex in particular had not bonded with his dad's new wife, and within the year, he started to refuse to visit their home for the weekend, as had previously been the pattern every fortnight. He felt uncomfortable in their house, especially around his dad's wife. Despite this, I felt that it was important for the boys to maintain a good relationship with their dad, and, to my regret, I forced Alex to keep up the visits for many months, thinking that this was the right thing for him. Eventually, after many tears and refusals, I realized how wrong I was and saw that this was cruel. Alex stopped going, and it was not long before Thomas became uncomfortable and also ceased his visits. As the boys' relationship with their dad deteriorated, both my ex-husband's sister and I wrote and tried to encourage him to see that the boys needed their dad in their lives in some way. However, he refused to talk about it and blocked my number, thus ceasing all contact with me, his children and his sister, who was only trying to help in a difficult situation. I do not want to comment further upon this, except to say that this hurt never left Alex. Although their broken relationship was not the reason he took his own life, it remained a deep sadness, about which he talked to me at length on the night of his 21st birthday. At the time of his death, Alex had had no contact whatsoever with his dad for nine years. Thomas had ceased contact some months after Alex, partly in solidarity with how he saw Alex being treated, and, subsequently, himself. That's not an easy decision to make when you are still only 11 and 14 years old.

Alex referenced this sad time in his final email to me and said that he had largely "found resolution" to past hurts. It was an unnecessary sadness that should never happen in any circumstance of divorce. I will never understand how a loving Dad – and he was for more than ten years – can walk away from his children, irrespective of whether his new wife wants them in their lives. I have never sought to absolve myself of any blame resulting in my marriage breakdown, but I believe that the failure of a marriage has many contributing factors that can only really be understood by the parties involved. No matter what happened, the priority should be ensuring that the children know how much they are valued. Both of my precious sons were at the heart of our new family dynamic, enjoying happy holidays and always knowing how much I loved them.

Alex and Tom's dad did not contact Tom or me when Alex died and has not in the three years and six months since Alex's death.

Despite such setbacks, Alex did enjoy many happy times, none more so than when he was able to indulge his passion for exploring new countries. He sought out local areas of interest while on family holidays – lying on a beach was never his thing as, like myself, Alex had fair skin and found sunbathing tedious. I first became impressed and slightly in awe of his adventurous spirit on a family holiday to Rome soon after Alex's 16th birthday. Whilst his siblings remained close to my husband and me as we went sightseeing in the hot, busy streets of Rome, Alex asked if he could go off on his own, navigating the Roman underground and meeting us back in the evenings, to which we agreed after some anxious consideration. He had a wonderful time exploring the labyrinth of ancient streets to seek out the heart of the city – its people, its history. He even took us back to try out his finds: the best pizza restaurant in an unimposing side street that we would never have stumbled across and the best gelato shop in Rome. Alex had unlocked his inner explorer, and his love of travel and discovery of different countries and cultures never left him. Alex impressed his English teacher on his return by writing about his adventures in Rome and, aged 16, produced an article that his English teacher still uses as an exemplar piece of writing, describing Alex as "an emerging writer of such promise."

"… There were ancient Roman artefacts littered like Coke cans… equally discarded and unvalued. The new perfectly fuses with the traditional; terracotta roof tiles, sun-bleached walls and shutters… your ears are bombarded with high-pitched horns and two-stroke Vespa engines… this city is unique and provides a totally spellbinding experience that I will never forget."

I am reminded here to mention that, following Alex's death, his head teacher and A level English teacher created an annual award in his honour for the most promising creative writer in the sixth form. James and I were present when they named the first recipient of the Alex Hardy Creative Writing Shield, and I will always remember both my pride and heartbreak.

As a 16-year-old, Alex suffered from teenage spots and, as he was so embarrassed by them, I took him to see a dermatologist who prescribed Roaccutane. Alex was on this treatment for a few months until his skin became clear, and he did not suffer again from this problem. I have since read of the dangerous psychological side effects that some attribute to this drug, such as depression, especially in young males, and possibly even suicide. However, I am not able to say with any conviction whether it could have been a contributing factor, as Alex completed this treatment seven years before his death.

Alex was especially practical and could mend anything, it seemed. I remember the time we had rented a holiday home in Austria when Alex was 15. The family was watching the Olympics on TV when we became aware of Alex cutting the grass, having found an old lawnmower! How typical of Alex, active and driven, yet content in his own company. The house we rented was on a steep hill, and Alex would cycle for a few miles each morning to collect our breakfast pastries, preferring to get up and enjoy an adventure in our foreign surroundings rather than lying in bed. It strikes me as I recall these memories that Alex's favourite pastime as a toddler was to push his plastic lawnmower behind his dad while he cut the grass, and, from the age of three, he was never far from his bike, whether it was his first plastic three-wheeler or his sophisticated mountain bike that came later. Cycling remained a lifelong passion for Alex, and he was able to enjoy this pastime in Canada.

Alex also became an accomplished cook who liked to experiment, often producing delicious results. The last time he came home in the year before his death, he cooked Steve and me a lovely meal that required no recipe, just his flair and knowledge of flavours. It took me more than three years after his death to be able to cook that dish again, and when I did, I could not eat it. The memory of Alex's pleasure in how much we enjoyed it is so painful. I can still see his contented, warm smile as we told him how delicious it tasted.

The only real friction at home during Alex's teenage years was his love of his PlayStation and the amount of time he dedicated to it – too much, in my opinion! Alex was a bright student, but he could not be accused of excessive studying. Despite this, he passed 11 GCSEs with mostly A and B grades, followed by three A levels two years later. By the age of 18, he had largely given up the PlayStation and spent most of his leisure time outdoors, becoming an expert skier and snowboarder, and an enthusiastic walker, cyclist and jogger in and around his new home in Canada.

When Alex was around 16, he exploited what he called "a gap in the market" and sold sweets and canned drinks at high school during break times, almost like a black marketer. He would source the items in multi-packs from local supermarkets, often drafting me in to acquire them during my weekly shop. I reluctantly agreed, as my husband thought Alex's plan was inspired and enterprising. Alex charged students the same price per item as they would pay in a store, which meant he doubled his money on every chocolate bar and can of pop that he carefully chose for maximum appeal. Alex earned a healthy profit of more than £1,000 before the school stepped in and closed down his little business.

Alex had a love of cars, and he knew the make of every car on the road by the age of five. As a teenager, his knowledge and love of sports and supercars exceeded even his stepdad's, and *Top Gear* was by far their favourite programme. Alex was a dedicated keeper of a "*Top Gear* Cool Wall", where he and Steve would assess and classify cars as "variously cool", "sub-zero" or "plain boring". It heartened me to see on one of our visits to Canada that Alex had stuck the Cool Wall to his fridge and maintained this link with home.

Alex and I mostly liked the same flavours, and this was especially so in our taste in cakes and ice cream. In later years, Alex developed a taste for vegan flavours, which I have never been able to enjoy – at least not yet. I am reminded of an impressive cake made for my birthday by a lovely friend a few months before Alex left for Canada. Both Tom and James were at school, and I recall Alex being at home as he had just finished his A levels. The cake was our favourite carrot flavour, and we both agreed it was one of the best homemade cakes either of us had tasted. It's a memory I now cherish, just Alex and me. I remember exactly where we were sitting, Alex's smile, what we said. I am grateful for my remarkable memory. I thought I would have a lifetime of such moments…

As I have mentioned, Alex was a bright student, especially gifted in English, which he took for A level and for which he had a place to study at university. Still, I knew that he was keen to explore the world, and so it came as no surprise that 18-year-old Alex deferred his university place and set off for Canada, a country he had fallen in love with during a school skiing trip several years earlier.

Alex's 6th birthday with Thomas – best pals and pirates

"Your children are not your children... You may house their bodies but not their souls, for their souls dwell in the house of tomorrow, which you cannot visit, not even in your dreams."

Kahlil Gibran

CHAPTER 3

LETTING GO

I do not think I knew how much I was committing to a lifetime of wearing my heart outside my body when I had children. When they were younger, it seemed infinitely easier to protect my boys from the hurt that at times accompanies growing up. But there eventually came a time when I had to let Alex and then Tom go to explore the world on their own terms, as I still believe that it enriches your life and helps you have a better understanding of the world before settling down.

Little did I know when I agreed for Alex to go on a school skiing trip to Canada at the age of 14 that the seed would be sown. Four years later, on 14 September 2012, I held him close as I hugged him goodbye at Manchester Airport for his supposed gap year in Canada. It was extremely difficult for me to let Alex go, but as this seemed to be the norm for young people of his age, and knowing Alex's love of travel and wish to show his independence, I had to agree. Of course, at the time I had no idea that in letting him go, in five more years, he would be gone forever.

How many times in the preceding months had I heard him say, "It's only for a year, Mum," but, deep down, I wondered if he would fall in love with his new country and extend his time away. The lure of the Rocky Mountains and an outdoor lifestyle were too tempting, and a place to study English at his first-choice university failed to create enough interest in Alex to choose that path for himself. If I did not know it for sure that day at the departure gate, I had to accept it during the five years that followed: my darling, long-awaited, wise, amusing and kind first-born had made a new life far away from home. After many tears – mine – Skype calls and several transatlantic visits, I reluctantly admitted that he had done the right thing. I loved visiting him in his new country and accepted that his outdoor, activity-packed lifestyle and Canada's can-do culture suited him perfectly. Alex fell in love with the mountains, the stunning scenery, the wilderness, the outdoor way of life and the skiing in winter and cycling trails in summer. Perhaps most of all, Alex felt at home among the warm and diverse people he met. He was recognized as competent, popular, kind, self-effacing and hard-working, and he achieved several promotions during his time there. He impressed colleagues at work with his intellect, empathy and ability to lighten stressful situations with his infectious grin and warm humour. Alex was happy living, working and enjoying his time amongst the most stunning scenery imaginable and said to me that the only downside to his decision to make his life in Canada was the geographical distance to me and his brothers.

It was, therefore, no surprise that Alex deferred his university place to study English and told me after that first year that he was deferring it again for another year. At this point it seemed unlikely that he would return to the UK to study, as he was earning his keep and loving his life in Canada. Alex was a Canadian resident at the time of his death and, had he lived, he would have undoubtedly become a Canadian citizen. Alex ultimately decided that university was not for him, and on my regular visits, I could see why he did not want to leave the life he had worked so hard to make for himself in the beautiful mountains that had become his home.

One year after Alex left to go to Canada, my husband's elderly father died. Douglas was an amenable, easy, sincere and uncomplicated man of whom we were all very fond. It was so typical of Alex's nature that, just a week after his 19th birthday, he needed no prompting to write the perfect message to his grieving stepdad. I include his words here as testament to Alex's kindness, now so especially poignant:

Hi Ste,

I know words can seem pointless at times like these, but I am sorry to hear about Douglas. He was a kind man who always treated me and Thomas well despite having no biological relation to us and our late entry into his life. I hope he passed peacefully and in no pain. I am sorry I can't be there to support you both now and at his funeral, but I will be thinking of you. Death is incredibly hard to deal with, but keep your chin up and remember the good times: it is what he would have wanted as the resilient man he was.

My thoughts go to you,
Alex
Xx

In subsequent phone calls around that time, I recall how particularly caring and loving Alex was. This seems especially moving when I reflect on how uncaring many have been since Alex's death, despite being decades older. Age is no guarantee of compassion or decency.

I went out to visit Alex in Canada several times: sometimes alone, sometimes with his brothers and Steve. I visited him on my own for his 21st birthday and took him on a holiday to Vancouver Island. We travelled there and back by sea plane, spent an afternoon whale watching and indulged in an afternoon tea and a birthday dinner. It was such a special time creating memories I now cherish. How proud I was as he introduced me to his many friends and colleagues during those visits, and how delighted I felt that my loving son seemed equally pleased for his friends to meet me.

One of the first things Alex and I always did together when either I arrived in Canada or he came home, was to indulge in our favourite ice cream, and I have many memories of us chatting over our frozen treats. On one of my visits to see Alex, I remember us sitting beside the beautiful turquoise lake near his flat, eating our favourite ice cream, and he shared with me that he would like one child in the future. Alex would have made a great dad, but sadly this will never happen now.

A beautiful memory that still hurts to re-visit is of a lovely walk Alex took me on during my visit alone to Canada to celebrate his 21st birthday. I can still hear Alex's words of encouragement when the heat of the day and the elevation of the climb through stunningly scenic woods made me ask how much further to our destination. He replied, "Mum, you can do this, not much further." His love for me on that day shone, and I feel acute pain as I remember how wonderful I felt. As the trees cleared, the view was absolutely stunning, as Alex had said it would be. We sat together on a huge boulder overlooking the lake, and after a while, a few other walkers arrived. Alex asked them to take a photograph of us with the beautiful turquoise lake and the majestic Rocky Mountains as a backdrop, and this is my favourite picture of Alex and me. We stood up, and Alex instinctively put his arm around me. I will never forget the ease with which Alex held me, and the closeness and love between us will stay with me always.

Several days after Alex's 21st birthday, he arranged for us to have a special dinner in a beautiful hotel. He arrived from his flat to pick me up in my hotel room and surprised me by complimenting me on my new pale pink linen dress. We arrived at the restaurant and were met by one of Alex's colleagues, who also paid me a nice compliment about my outfit. I remember the pride on Alex's face. Thank you, Adam. I will never throw that pink dress away, but I have been unable to wear it since due to the memory of that occasion and how it now belongs to that night.

During this visit, Alex spoke of the impact of his dad's decision to cease contact with him when he was 14 and said that he felt like a "worthless son." It hurt me so much to see the pain in Alex's eyes, and I tried to reassure him that despite his dad's actions, he had always loved Alex very much, and I was sure that this could not have changed in the nine years since they had seen each other. Alex explained that this sadness was buried deep inside him and that he had largely made peace with the hurt caused. I know that this is not why Alex took his own life, but it is nonetheless true that the sadness of his dad's absence never totally left him.

The following year I took Alex and James on a holiday on one of Alex's trips back to the UK. Tom was unable to come, as he was at university in Newcastle at that time. This was a year before Alex's death, and he seemed quieter than usual. I had a feeling that something was wrong, but he insisted he was fine and was very convincing. Tragically and unbeknownst to anyone at home or in Canada, Alex was suffering.

The uneasy feeling I had from our loving and deep conversation at his birthday dinner that evening on Victoria Island never totally left me. More happy memories of our time together would be made, but little did I know, time on this earth with my gorgeous first-born son was running out…

Alex and James, Glacier Lake, Canada 2014. They flew in by seaplane – a special treat!

Alex and brown bears, Canada 2015

"…There's no way to know the exact second your life changes forever. You can only begin to know that moment by looking in the rear-view mirror. And trust me when I tell you that you never, ever see it coming."

Anthony Ray Hinton, *The Sun Does Shine*

CHAPTER 4

WHEN TIME STOPPED

I had planned to visit Alex in the autumn of 2017, but in October, my youngest son James broke his wrist whilst playing in a football match and required surgery. This meant that my plans were postponed until his cast was removed. Alex completely understood this, and I had no reason to doubt his insistence that I did not leave his younger brother when he needed me at home. How I wish I had known that when the cast was removed six weeks later, it would be too late…

In retrospect, I now wonder if Alex was trying to say goodbye to me in our final phone call six days before he took his own life. With the benefit of hindsight, several things he said to me might have hinted at that, but it was so subtle. Plus, I knew I was going to visit him in Canada the following week, and I thought our deeper conversations could take place then, face to face, but, tragically, that was not to be. Alex was his usual loving self during that phone call, perhaps even more so. He was clever, indistinct and shrewdly threw me off any scent, swatting away any concerns I had when I asked how he really was. Still, I had an instinct that I cannot easily narrate, almost like a sixth sense, an unease, a gut feeling, an ominous cloud despite his warm and chatty conversation, which lasted for over an hour.

It was 7pm on a Saturday evening, 25 November 2017, when we were disturbed by a knock on the front door. A policeman in a high-visibility jacket had come to end my happy world, eviscerating my life as I knew it. As I write, I can recall now this sound, this primal screaming coming out of my mouth as I fell to the floor, but it did not register as being from me. I now know that this was the sound of my heart breaking. Poor James, only ten years of age, was standing beside me in shocked silence as the world seemed to stop. Did nobody know that I could not survive this level of pain? I begged whoever in the universe was listening to immediately retract those words. With a lack of compassion, the policeman went on to say, "I know it's not the best of news..." They were the first but, sadly, not the last unbelievably insensitive words I would have to face. Everything was surreal, and it was almost like being unconscious, numb as though anesthetized, and outside of my body. I felt like I was falling into a gap between two worlds – my old one and the new, unwelcome one into which I was thrown, forced to inhabit for the rest of my days. I was inconsolable, and in my heart, I still am.

Part of me died that night and will never return. Alex's tragic suicide made me a member of the horrific club no parent wants to join: that of a bereaved parent and, more specifically, a bereaved parent of a child who has died by suicide. I read recently that no Hollywood film has ever captured the true depth of pain in a mother's scream when told that her beloved child is dead. I now know this to be true. How do you make sense of the unthinkable when you're enjoying an ordinary Saturday evening with your family? I could not absorb what my ears were hearing. If I had had a gun, I would have put it to my head and pulled the trigger. I wanted to die, to be with Alex. My heart broke and can never be mended. My brain could not compute the shocking news and now, more than three years later, there are times when it still seems so horrifyingly unreal. I was screaming and felt that I could still reverse this shocking news by telling the policeman to stop talking, as though willing it not to be true could make it so. Could I rewind and delete the moment he uttered those life changing, traumatizing words? "Are you Lesley Roberts? Can I come in? Alex... has passed away."

When I lost him, I lost the will to live, and a large part of me stopped living, too. Thoughts of killing myself to be with Alex flitted through my mind. I just wanted to be with him. It would not have mattered if I had 20 children, my brain just wanted to be with the one who was now lost to me forever, if only for another minute, another hug, another shared moment, another shared smile…

Oh my God, my beautiful boy, what have you done?

The policeman left after giving Steve the number for the Foreign and Commonwealth Office in London. Alex had died nine or ten hours earlier, and it had taken that much time for the news to reach me in the UK. To this day I dislike the phrase "passed away", especially when referring to an untimely, tragic and shocking death. It sounds like an almost pleasant state to me, rather than the cold, hard reality that comes with "has died" or "is dead". These phrases more accurately describe the brutality and hell for parents left behind after their child's death.

I was grateful that Steve took charge, speaking to the FCO and, later, British Airways to book the first available flight to Vancouver. All I kept repeating was, "Tom, get Tom, please get Tom," who was in Newcastle for the last six months of his biology degree. Steve put James to bed and left for Newcastle. Thankfully, James slept solidly through the night.

I called a friend, screaming incoherently that Alex was dead. She arrived at my house, stayed an hour and left. I needed to be alone in my shell-shocked brain as I tried to compute the information. My body had its own way of processing the nightmare news of my beloved son's death, and I spent the following eight hours either in the bathroom or silently sitting on my bed, staring at the wall in complete shock. I think I knew even then that if I started crying, my screams would have woken the neighbourhood and, more importantly, my poor little ten-year-old, asleep until he woke to face his new reality, that of a bereaved brother facing the rest of his life without the sibling he loved so very much.

Time lost meaning as I waited for Steve to return with Tom. I sat alone, mute, unable to move, completely traumatized. It tortured me that I was not with Alex when he took his last breath, as I had been when he took his first. I have often thought since that horrendous night, *If Alex was going to die, I envy those parents whose child takes their last breath and dies in their arms.* How appalling does that sound, envying people who get to hold and kiss their children as they die from an illness or after an accident? But it is truly how I feel and felt then. I was lost in my own dark world, no longer a part of my previous one, and yet the clock was still ticking. How could that be when my whole world had just ended? How could a life that I loved more than my own cease to exist?

It seemed like only a short time between Steve leaving for Newcastle and him arriving back with Tom sometime around 4am. I met them at the front of the house, where only nine hours earlier my life as I knew it had ended. I silently fell into my dear Tom's arms as he walked through the door, something that his big brother would never do again. I could not speak, and he just held me tight. Tom, my lovely middle son, bereaved as he was, simply knew what to say: "It's all right mum, I am here now." Out of everything I have written for this book, that quote, my clear memory of Tom's bravery and the unspoken emotion of that moment between us always brings a lump to my throat. Tom and I did not need words – there weren't any. He led me to the sofa, and we sat in collective shock. How proud Alex would have been of Tom, who has proven to be the most loving and wonderful support to me and his little brother. My husband Steve is a caring and steady presence for Tom, James and me, too. Still, the strong, deep emotional connection that binds Tom and I – most especially to our dear Alex – is my greatest comfort.

I learnt the devastating reasons for Alex's suicide on the evening of his death in a long and loving email I received from him, which he had timed to arrive in my inbox some ten hours after his death. It took an hour less for the Foreign and Commonwealth Office and the Cheshire police to deliver the news of his death to me. As Alex kept his private anguish to himself, none of his suffering was known to any of his family or friends.

Alex, at the age of 21, had visited his GP in Canada, as he was suffering from a painful condition called phimosis. I discovered that Alex had been referred to a urologist, and he recommended a circumcision.

He explained to Alex that this was a routine procedure, and scant reference was made to the possible risks. Alex's laptop had broken, and he was uncomfortable researching such a delicate procedure in the public library. Confiding in no one, he put his trust in the urologist and proceeded with the surgery. He wrote subsequently that he had a deep feeling of unease about this doctor and did not like his abrupt, arrogant manner. Sadly, I subsequently discovered that this surgeon had many dissatisfied and damaged patients, although, in the interest of balance, he also has those who were pleased with the outcome of their surgery. Had I or Alex known of these mixed reviews, we would have been deeply concerned, and it is unlikely that Alex would have proceeded with the operation, especially not with this surgeon.

Alex wrote that he knew immediately that surgery had been a catastrophic mistake. Over the next two years, Alex sought advice from other doctors and healthcare professionals on how to remedy the pain and dysfunction. However, he understood that his surgery could not be reversed, and there was no cure. Alex killed himself at the age of 23.

I will never be the same as I was before, and I now view my life in two parts: before and after Alex died. My body was in shock for hours, days and weeks, even, and I think that the total shock has still not completely left me. In those early days, the shock provided some degree of protection, as I was unable to fully grasp the enormity of Alex's death and my horrific new life without him. The pain is so deep that it is like an amputation, an emotional amputation. In fact, I would have much preferred, given a choice that night, to undergo an amputation, or even better, I would have given my own life without hesitation if it had brought my dear son back. That desire to change places remains the case today, if only it were possible. I cared not a jot if I lived or died and saw death as preferable if it would bring me close to Alex. Still, even in those desperate hours following the news, something deep within me knew that I owed it to Tom and James to live my life for as long as I could. I had to be to the best, strong, loving mum I could be as they navigated this new, painful terrain. My boys needed me, and I needed them.

James was ten years old when Alex died, and Tom was twenty, so, naturally, they each had a unique relationship with their big brother due to their different ages and memories. Of course, Tom knew all the facts of our nightmare, but it wasn't the same for James, who was bewildered and shocked and needed age-appropriate information at that time. Over the past three years, we have answered his questions as they have arisen, and he now knows all that he wants to. As James was so young, he had less memory of Alex to draw on, and this protected him to an extent, which was not the case for Tom. Suffice it to say that the devastating loss of their beloved brother had a massive impact on both boys. Through love and strength, they are dealing with their loss admirably and have made Alex proud, no doubt. The strong bond between Tom and James brings me such comfort.

Alex left loving letters for Tom, James and me when he died, but James' was the only one that he had hand-written and left beside his body. The rest were sent by email, which at ten years old, James did not use, and I believe that is just how Alex wanted it. The letters were beautiful, explaining what had brought him to this place of despair in an age-appropriate way for each of his brothers. I will be forever grateful to my darling, 6-foot-2, kind, gentle, intelligent, witty, eloquent, thoughtful, self-effacing, modest, handsome son for trying so hard in these messages to attempt to care for us after his death.

Suicide is different from other deaths. We, the survivors, cannot blame an accident or a terrible, terminal disease. Instead, we grieve for the very person who has taken our loved one's life. I torture myself that I failed to save my darling boy. Perhaps in time I will learn to forgive myself for not keeping him alive, that I will come to accept that, at 23 years old, it was Alex's decision to end his life, and he deliberately chose to exclude me from his private suffering, despite sharing many happy and loving moments with me. Of course, I have endlessly revisited and scrutinized the memories of the last time I saw Alex alive, our last holiday together – the laughs and conversations we had shared. What did I miss? I am not the only one in my family convinced that Alex's caring nature and love for me meant that he shielded me from his pain, naively believing that he was protecting me. I will never know for how long Alex had planned his death and can only guess with the facts and feelings I have. Hindsight is a wonderful thing. If only I had booked my flight to Canada a week earlier. If only he had waited for me, if only…

Again, hindsight is my constant enemy. In Alex's final year alive, I was not the only one who detected a subtle change in him. I learnt afterwards that his friends and colleagues thought they, too, might have missed some signs that all was not quite right with him. Alex was always popular, and he enjoyed socializing without being the centre of attention. A few close friends told me in the days following his death that, in his last few months, the light that had shone in his eyes and his infectious grin had both seemed dimmed. I had also noticed this, but when I tried to ask Alex about how he really was, I was met with a wall of reassurances that all was okay, and I was worrying about nothing. I longed for this to be true, yet as my husband now reminds me, during those last months – and, to a lesser extent, the whole time Alex lived in Canada – I would often wake in the night saying his name. I think I had an instinct, a premonition, a feeling deep inside myself that I could not understand or fully articulate. It was as though my subconscious fears knew that tragedy lay ahead, but I did not, could not, know, and Alex was a good enough actor to allay my concerns. I can see his gorgeous grin and smiling eyes even now as I write these words. He would be thinking, *Typical Mum, she knew me too well, I did not convince her.* I am now certain that this crossed his mind whenever I asked him, and I will never forgive myself for failing to act on my unease. My husband Steve will not mind me saying that he often rolled his eyes at me while saying, "Alex is fine, you are always worrying about him." A mother's instinct is a powerful force – ignore it at your peril.

"Often the hardest person to forgive is yourself."
Charlie Mackesy, The Boy, the Mole, the Fox and the Horse

A final word about hindsight, useless though it is: something about our last telephone conversation continues to haunt me. Alex did not want to get off the phone that evening and was especially chatty and loving. When I hung up, I was pleased that I was going to be with him in Canada the following week. I also felt relieved that James had just had the cast removed from his broken wrist, and the operation to mend it had been a success, thus allowing me to visit Alex more easily. The tragedy is that I did, indeed, arrive in Canada within days of that call, but not for our usual happy times. We should have visited our favourite gelato shop – where we often chose the same flavour, honeycomb – or our favourite café, where we both liked the sour cherry scone. We should have had our favourite lakeside and mountain walks, our laughs, our hugs and special moments just being together. Instead, I travelled to Canada to sit beside my darling son's body as he lay in his coffin.

"The hardest part of losing a child is living every day afterwards."

Anonymous

CHAPTER 5

RETURNING TO CANADA

The pain of returning to Canada knowing that it was now too late to see my darling son alive was almost too much for my broken heart to bear. I would have thought that the human body could not possibly cope with such extreme pain, and I would have preferred to have succumbed to the agony and quietly joined my lovely boy instead. I did survive the trip – sadly, for how I felt at the time – and perhaps am still alive only because I recognized my responsibility to be the best mum to both Tom and James. They deserve me to be present in their lives and to help them live with our tragedy. Perhaps, in time, I will find some peace, some moments of happiness again. I do know though that Alex hoped for me to be strong for myself and for his brothers.

Steve and I were met with only kindness by the British Airways staff at both Manchester and Heathrow Airports, as well as in Vancouver on our return. They just had to look at me to see the shock and devastation. Alex would have been pleased to know that we were upgraded to business class and were able to lie down for the long flight. In happier circumstances, the tasty food, drinks and comfortable seats would have been much enjoyed, but they were all lost on us. I was mute for the whole journey. I will never forget the kindness of the head flight attendant Daniel on the flight from London to Vancouver. His calming manner and warmth helped me to lie down, even though I was numb with grief. I hoped the floor of the plane would open so that I could silently slide out among the clouds and cease to be. That way, I would not have to face the horrors that I knew awaited me in Canada.

I spent a sleepless first night in Canada despite the comfort of a beautiful room, which Alex's employer had provided for our stay. The following morning, we met with the directors of the company where he had worked, and they offered any help we might need. They provided a car to drive us to the Chapel of Rest in the neighbouring town to see my darling Alex in his temporary, plain, wooden coffin. The following evening, they organized a reception for Alex's colleagues and friends – several of whom I had met on previous visits – so that they could offer their condolences. A car was also at our disposal so I could visit Alex's flat. The police had sealed it off until my arrival, which allowed me to retrieve any personal belongings that I wanted to bring home to Cheshire. It was all surreal and, although I was present in attending to all that needed to be done, I was numb.

As previously mentioned, I have an extremely good memory and, despite my shock, I can recall every agonizing moment since hearing of Alex's death. I know Alex would have sniggered at my struggle to climb into the vehicle provided to go and see him. Many of the cars in Canada are enormous SUVs and, although I am of medium height, the hike to climb in took me by surprise, and I remember almost falling out as I attempted to do so. Alex would have no doubt seen the dark humour in that. Was he playing his part to lighten my mood, if only for a second? Was his presence making itself known? I cannot explain how close I felt my darling Alex beside me as I navigated my way through my worst days on this earth. Again, I could not speak on the journey. All too soon, we were met at the Chapel of Rest entrance by a lovely man who offered his condolences to me and explained that he was the funeral director.

Time has not obliterated a single second of the next hour from my memory, and I know it never will. I needed to see my darling boy, to be with him, to grasp the enormity and horror and permanence of our tragedy. I recall every touch, every word and emotion of those gut-wrenching but precious moments that reunited me with my dead son. I remember the silence of the large room, except for the soft music playing in the background; the raised altar at the front; and a large screen depicting my darling son's name, written in italic script and set against a backdrop of the beautiful, snow-capped mountains he loved so much. As I approached the altar upon which the open coffin of my beautiful boy lay, I heard wailing. I think it was me.

Until that very moment of seeing my darling Alex in his coffin – a sight no mother should ever have to see – nothing seemed real. Except now it was. His perfect face looked like he was asleep. I gently placed my hand in his, but it was so cold. I leant over him and kissed his forehead. I spent precious time talking to him, sobbing quietly, begging for this not to be true. I told my special, courageous, kind, wonderful boy how much I loved him and asked how I could possibly live without him. I said that he was too good for this world, and I needed to be with him. Could I be with him? I welcomed death as a release from this agony and clearly remember feeling the urge to climb into the coffin beside him and remain there forevermore.

I cut a small lock of hair from his forehead, and this is my most treasured possession, which I keep beside my bed in an engraved silver heart-shaped box I bought on my return home. I will forever be grateful to the owner of the Chapel of Rest in Canada for his gentle care in my desperate state, somehow knowing for how long to leave me alone with Alex and when to return – the right man in the right job. My husband Steve showed his love and care for me by providing strength in the background of my agony. He respected that, as Alex's mum, I was alone in my shock and grief and was largely incapable of speech during those first days in Canada. Nobody could know the depths of pain to which my soul had sunk as I saw my beloved, beautiful boy in his coffin. It was beyond words to tear myself away from Alex knowing that the next time I saw him would be at our local funeral home in Cheshire after his repatriation.

Again, we returned to the hotel in silence. I simply had no words, but I found some escape in writing as Steve, a constantly comforting presence by my side, made me a cup of tea. In those early days of hell in Canada, my writing took the form of emails, a safe place to pour out my internal agony, mostly to my family at home. The replies

I received sustained me as I felt their love from across the Atlantic. They were willing me to survive this week of horror and, until my last breath on earth, every second of that week will never, ever leave me.

The following morning, we had to prepare for the visit to the local police station to retrieve Alex's personal effects, including the wallet I gave him some years earlier, which contained his bank cards, driving licence and Canadian residency card. There was also an unexpected envelope containing the only handwritten note to his little brother James. This note was found next to his body, and below is a part of that most precious message:

> *Wherever you are, wherever I am – remember Alex loves you.*
> *You should not be sad because I love you so much forever.*
> *Whenever you see the brightest star in the sky, remember it is me watching you, and I will always be with you.*

This beautiful note from my first-born son to my youngest son touches my soul every time I read it. The heartfelt words, so lovingly chosen by Alex, must have been excruciating for him to write. I can close my eyes and be beside him in that moment, and they are the words I would imagine he would write to James. He tried so hard for two years to make the outcome of his story different, and I am certain that was largely because of his love and concern for his little brother. Tragically, Alex could see no other path for himself.

I asked to meet the police officer who had attended Alex and attempted CPR to no avail – it was already too late. When she entered the room, my jaw dropped. I simply could not believe what I was seeing. The police officer was only a few years older than Alex and strikingly similar in looks, down to the same large, expressive green eyes. It was uncanny. She was professional and friendly but clearly extremely moved and struggling as she expressed her sympathy. I sobbed and thanked her for all that she had tried to do and for her genuine concern, so obvious in her eyes whilst I remarked on the extraordinary similarity in her and Alex's looks. Steve agreed that there was a striking resemblance. She apologized that she had not been able to save him, and I wept and told her it was not her fault, and that Alex would not have wanted her to suffer in any way as a result of his actions. He was so caring and would be appalled if she did. I asked her what her name was. "Alex," she replied. For the rest of my life, I will remain astounded at this coincidence.

The following day, Steve and I went to Alex's flat with the empty holdall I had brought from home to retrieve some of my son's belongings knowing that one day – not yet – his brothers would want their own keepsakes to treasure. Strangely, for myself, I thought that Alex was with me and always would be, as I had no intention of letting him go. I felt that this was not really happening and, therefore, I was cocooned in my belief that none of this was real. Needless to say, going through Alex's flat was yet another agonizing task, not least because I had visited Alex there several times, and it was where he had chosen to end his life. Additionally, many of Alex's possessions were clothes I had bought for him both in Canada and the UK: the ski jacket we had chosen together on one of my visits that hung on the coat hook; the blue suede shoes and Vans I had bought him in Chester on his last visit home; the fruit bowl and garlic press we had picked out while shopping in Canada; his skis; and many other items familiar to me. Torture. I asked his friends to choose anything they wanted from everything that was left and asked that the rest to go to charity. Alex's flatmate chose my son's fancy ice cream machine, as Alex had recently taught him how to make his favourite treat. He had developed a refined interest in food and was passionate about clean eating. He had also become quite a connoisseur of wines and spirits, especially whisky.

I am reminded of an occasion on one of Alex's visits home when he tried to encourage me to supplement my favourite Mary Berry cake recipes with the trend for natural, raw or vegan ingredients, such as coconut oil, avocados, seeds and, of course, Canadian maple syrup. To aid my conversion, Alex had presented me with a cookbook entitled *Rawsome Vegan Baking*, and so, on one of his visits home, I bought the exotic, unusual and expensive ingredients in order to show my culinary flexibility. The results were not especially enjoyed by any of us, so Alex decided to take matters into his own hands and bake some raw, vegan cakes. He grinned his gorgeous grin and shook his head when, after a single bite of a cacao nib and avocado brownie, I confessed that it was one of the worst cakes I had ever put in my mouth. We laughed and laughed. However, we did enjoy his amazing salads and healthy, tasty snacks – all produced with flair and panache. Alex ate exceptionally well in Canada and loved cooking using the healthiest ingredients, especially enjoying avocado, kale, quinoa, chia seeds and a variety of nuts, beans and pulses. He rarely ate meat and was always able to concoct a tasty meal whilst never giving up his love of the best gelato he could find. Probably his favourite food was Japanese sushi; again, not something I enjoy, but a fondness he shared with his brother Tom. On one of our family visits to see Alex, he and Tom went together to a sushi restaurant, and I know that this is now a cherished memory for Tom. I cannot see the day when I will be able to bake from that vegan cookbook, as it is just too painful, so, for now, it remains in a special place: a wardrobe containing my darling son's personal items that I treasure. These include his favourite cuddly toy as a toddler – a giraffe – and assorted belongings that meant something to Alex, including the sweatshirt he wore when he last hugged me tightly and said, "It won't be too long, Mum, when we see each other again." If only I had known, I would never have released my grip.

As I have mentioned, Alex and I shared a passion for ice cream, and we always had the same favourite flavour. We also loved the same kinds of cakes: lemon, pineapple, ginger, banana, carrot, orange, poppyseed, coffee, coconut, cherry and almond. Despite both having a healthy love of chocolate, it was our least preferred cake flavour. On my first – and every subsequent – visit to Canada, we always went to our favourite coffee and cake shop and ordered the same treat: a sour cherry scone. Alex and I loved them and always bought one each to enjoy while sitting in the wooden seats by a nearby stream. Following Alex's death, I was drawn to our favourite shop. I tentatively approached the counter and ordered our favourite scones before the tears started to fall. I have no idea why I was ordering them, as I certainly couldn't eat one and doubt I ever will again. I explained to the friendly assistant about Alex's death, and she visibly crumpled and said, "Oh no, not the handsome jogger who often bought the sour cherry scone, the polite Brit with the amazing smile…" She was yet another Canadian upon whom Alex had made an impression. I brought both of those scones back home to the UK with me, and they remained in our freezer for many months, as nobody could bring themselves to eat them. They were eventually thrown away.

On the night of Alex's death, he had met some friends in a local bar. I felt compelled to visit this bar, and, as I stood in the doorway, tears rolled down my face. I was so overwhelmed that this was where Alex had spent his last hours. I said nothing, but a barman and young woman saw me, and realizing who I was, said, "Alex's mom." They came from behind the bar and engulfed me in a hug. Everyone I met was so warm, so caring, so sad for the loss of their friend, my son.

The penultimate day in Canada was to be spent with Alex's friends, but first I had to arrange to pick up his death certificate before I flew home, as it was needed for Alex's body to be repatriated. The local coroner, in conjunction with the local police, could not have been more helpful in speeding up the process. They arranged to have the document, the one that no parent ever wants to receive, hand-delivered to our hotel room at 5am by one of Alex's colleagues. I was not sleeping, spending the nights propped up in bed staring into the dark and, therefore, I heard the dreaded envelope as it slid under our hotel room door. I stood in the early dawn light, staring at the nondescript brown package on the floor, aware of the horrific document that lay within. I tentatively picked it up and slowly opened it. It stared back at me, edged in black, unlike his birth certificate that was thousands of miles away at home and outlined in red. Again, I was mute, dazed, screaming inside, trying to stand, yet feeling another punch being delivered as I saw my lovely son's name on this most shocking of documents. The pain inside me escalated even higher than I thought possible. I firmly believed that I would soon die, as the pain I was experiencing was surely not survivable.

The final evening in Canada was spent meeting around 60 of Alex's friends and colleagues at a reception organized by Alex's employer. I had met several of his closest friends on previous visits to see Alex, although not all of them. This event proved to be extremely emotional, not only for me, but for those present, as they had just lost a friend and colleague in the most tragic of circumstances. They were such a warm and wonderful group of people, giving their time to share stories of times spent with Alex and shedding tears for our loss. I was comforted by the compassion in that room, by the wonderful colleagues and friends who came together to share their memories of my son. We all felt the weight of sadness at the end of a promising young life. Maintaining my composure as I addressed the silent room required every ounce of courage and love for my darling Alex that I had. You could have heard a pin drop as I told them a little about Alex's life in the UK before he met them in Canada. I talked from the heart about my lovely boy and will forever remember their warmth and tears. I think I did justice to my son as they listened to stories of his childhood and teenage years and joined some dots in the life of the young man they had taken into their hearts.

Some mentioned to me that they felt dreadful that Alex had not shared his suffering with them, despite having an enjoyable night out together only a few days before his death. I was told that, unusually for Alex, he had hit the dance floor and had a lovely time, dancing for hours. I asked them not to feel in any way guilty for Alex's death, for not knowing of his suffering, as none of us did, and he had written to them all to say just that. He explained to them, in his typically kind and thoughtful way, that he had wanted to end his life, but that he wished for all of them to remember him with a smile and not tears. Many stories were shared that night, and I will cherish them forever, as for me, too, blanks were filled in regarding Alex's life in Canada, and I was so proud to hear the many, many wonderful tales and comments about my beloved son.

One lovely girl around the same age as Alex approached me in tears and gave me Alex's beanie hat, which I treasure and keep beside my bed, often burying my head in it. She explained that the previous weekend a group of them had been out and walked home on an especially cold evening. She had no hat, and Alex lent his to her, typically generous of him. She was devastated that she was returning it to me and not to him.

One slightly older man came up to me, struggling to hold back his tears as he told me that my son was a thoughtful soul. This man said that he was the janitor where Alex worked. He explained that his position in the organization was low-ranking, yet each time Alex saw him, he would remember to enquire about the janitor's new-born son. Again, so typical of Alex, who always treated those he met with the same respect regardless of their position.

Another story I heard that night was about a regular wine and cheese evening, where it was, of course, usual to bring either a bottle of wine or some cheese. Alex had, however, arrived with a watermelon. This was described by his friends as "typically quirky, creative or goofy" of Alex, and I was told that, from then on, such evenings would always include someone bringing a watermelon in his memory.

A colleague of Alex's told me how they had asked him what he had done on a recent day off, and he replied, "Nothing much." It eventually came to light that Alex had driven for several hours to Vancouver and back so he could deliver coats that had been collected for the homeless, as nobody else had found the time to drop them off. His friends said that this was typical of Alex's kindness, humanity, modesty and compassion for others less fortunate than himself. The coats were of no use unless given to those in need, and he told no one of his charitable act. If Alex could alleviate suffering, he would try to do so, and if a task needed doing, he would just get on and do it.

I was told by his friends in Canada that he was never ill, even after a "heavy" night out. (Alex was sociable but generally preferred outings in a small group.) On one occasion, though, after a particularly heavy night out, Alex was discovered the following morning with his apartment key in his hand, sleeping soundly outside his front door – in a heated corridor, thankfully! Putting the key in its lock had obviously proved too tricky…

"All I can say about Alex is that he was a lovely person to work with. I remember when I trained him, he was very kind, respectful, polite and gentle. Alex was a quiet person, but smart and observant. Every time I was around Alex, I saw his big smile. It was my pleasure to see you, Alex's mum, today."

"Alex was a great young man, humorous, intelligent, passionate and curious. He was an active part of this amazing community. Let's make sure to celebrate him and remember him and all the moments we shared with him throughout the last five years."

Listed below are some of the adjectives used to describe Alex both on that evening and in many emails I subsequently received. These words still bring tears to my eyes, and I know he would have had no idea how much love there was for him from these wonderful people. He was variously described as: kind; super smart; the intelligent Brit who helped us with our complex visa applications; the guy who got things done; hard-working; reliable; sensitive; eloquent; knowledgeable; humorous and sarcastic; caring; gentle; observant; witty; goofy; a rocket on skis; smiling eyes; a grin that could light up the room; intuitive; empathetic; wouldn't hurt a fly; determined; the most intelligent guy I know.

Another described how Alex would keep his cool on especially hectic days, mentally sorting out orders when others would have panicked. A lovely Irish friend of Alex's called Stephen, who was especially kind to me after Alex died and who I remembered Alex particularly liked, said, "I wish he could have known how much we loved and respected him."

In particular I include here a part of the email I received from Alex's favourite roommate, a New Zealander named Cameron who shared a flat with Alex for around a year and who I enjoyed meeting on a couple of my visits. He now works in Bermuda. He wrote:

... The evening was a really nice opportunity to celebrate the life of such an amazing person and that everyone had fond memories of their friendship with Alex. I have copied a letter at the bottom that I put in a bottle and

released into the ocean out here in Bermuda. I would generally associate Alex with the mountains, and I would have loved to set this letter free at the top of a mountain but, unfortunately, Bermuda doesn't have any.

One of the key things is Alex and I shared so many of the same passions. I remember renting a car for a night to drive down to Vancouver on the beautiful Sea to Sky highway, and he was in control of music while I drove. Every song he played I instantly loved, and I'm quite picky with what I listen to. We had the day off together, and he came out of his room and said, "It's a nice day for a drive. Shall we hire a car and drive to Vancouver? There's a new bottle of bourbon at a boutique liquor store I want to try." Of course, I said yes – any chance to do that drive to Vancouver because it's so beautiful. We booked a room in Vancouver, and they upgraded us to a suite for some reason – wasn't complaining at all. Alex and I share a love for quality food and a well-made cocktail, so on this night we spent in Vancouver, we went on a tour of some of the best restaurants and bars in the city and met one of my good friends who knows the area really well. It was a truly amazing night, with Alex and I chatting continuously, which is a good sign of a quality friendship. I must say, I had quite the headache the next morning. Alex was loved by everyone!

In the letter he put in the bottle and sent out to sea, Cam wrote:

To my jungle brother,

Alex, I'm sorry to have you gone, bro. I had the pleasure of living with you for the better part of a year, and you were the perfect person for me to live with. You were generous, intelligent, creative, sociable, and your smile would light up the darkest of rooms. Coming home to freshly baked goods or a meal that you had been working on all day was a delight to my senses. Electro music would be cranking in the living room, and our fridge would be full of a range of delicious beers, or there would be a quality bourbon or wine sitting on our living room table. It's incredible how many people you meet through life, and how rare it is to find someone that has the same passions as you, and I found that in you. I have only found these passions and similarities in a few people, and I can't express how happy I am that I got to share these passions with you. You really were an extraordinarily amazing person, and, unfortunately, it takes something like this to fully appreciate someone's full amazingness. I will always remember our late-night movie sessions and music jamming sessions, where we would drink multiple quality beers, eat delicious food and chat 'til the early hours.

Your love for great food and drinks, music and the mountains replicate some of my strongest passions, and I'm so thrilled that I got to share these moments with you, like our restaurant tour of Vancouver or when we went to see Cyantific. It's nights like those that I will always remember, especially when I found you passed out outside our door with your keys in your hand. You were misunderstood by some but loved and cherished by so many people who cared about you. I found our personalities to be very similar, and this is probably why we got along so well. You found friends and family in Canada that miss you like you wouldn't imagine. I miss you and as unfortunate as this situation is, you have really made me appreciate what I have and the people that are around me.

Much love,
Cam

My broken heart was bursting with pride as I absorbed these lovely descriptions and stories of my wonderful son. My heartfelt thanks to all of Alex's friends and colleagues for their warmth and generosity, particularly Cameron, Stephen and, of course, Guillaume. Alex had made an impact on his many special friends and colleagues in Canada, and a few are in touch with me even now. I am so grateful to you, and I know Alex would thank you for the kindness you have shown to his mum.

The memories shared that night gave me the strength to face the coming days as we returned to the UK knowing that the son who I adored would soon be returning home in the cargo hold of another plane. Truly horrific.

"If ever there comes a day when we can't be together, keep me in your heart, I'll stay there forever."

Winnie the Pooh

CHAPTER 6

LETTING GO FOREVER

Letting go of my darling son is not yet a possibility for me. Alex will forever occupy the space in my heart that was always his, and I focus on the presence I feel – the presence of him being close to me – to survive this tragedy. Feeling connected to my son helps me, and as I would say to any other parent facing this nightmare, you must allow yourself to feel whatever you feel if it helps you survive, regardless of advice from those that cannot know, however well-intentioned their suggestions may be.

Alex's funeral was held a week before Christmas 2017. I chose the 14th, as he had been born on the 14th of July, and, somehow, this seemed right – except nothing about this was right. It was all so horrifically, tragically wrong. The funeral director in Canada had been kind and considerate, and I will always be grateful to him. If ever it were true that Alex was helping me through those hellish days back in Cheshire, then he sent me an angel in the form of Nigel, the local funeral director. Nigel was simply wonderful, the perfect man for the job, and without whom I truly do not believe I could have survived my darkest days on this earth. I am still in touch with him to this day. I know that Nigel was moved by Alex's death. Those few weeks before the funeral included such horrors as selecting a coffin for my adorable son. As soon as I saw the coffin in a brochure – who knew such grisly things existed? – I knew which one to have. It was painted with a lone skier set against a snowy mountain bathed in sunlight. This felt fitting for the life Alex had chosen. His name was inscribed on the end, and my heart broke some more as I confirmed each tiny detail of the funeral arrangements.

To choose the clothes for Alex's final journey was perhaps the most excruciating of everything that I had to deal with. I hope he would have approved of my selections; I think he would. The evening before the funeral, Steve and I took Tom to see his brother for the last time. I also wanted to be with my precious boy again following his repatriation. And I needed to, because it would be the very last time – I would never again be able to see him, touch him or kiss him. I had been unsure if this was the right thing for Tom, but he was of an age where it had to be his decision. I know that he won't mind me saying that, on seeing his big brother in his coffin, his first word as he took a slight step back was an expletive. I had already seen Alex in his coffin in Canada and was just desperate to be with him again, but Tom fled the room after only a minute or two because it was unbearable for him. I drank in Alex's gorgeous, handsome face for the last time. It was so cold but so peaceful, so somewhere else, and yet still so much my baby – just exactly himself, as though he was sleeping. I could have stayed with him forever.

In readiness for the funeral, Steve put together a slideshow of my favourite photographs of Alex to be shown before the service. I vaguely remember helping him to select the photographs, each image a dagger of memories to my heart. I could barely look at them, such was the pain. I clearly recall this being another horrific task that took every ounce of courage I could summon: poring over the happy photographs of my smiling, beautiful boy who I would never see again.

In the days leading up to the funeral, I had to select the music to be played. I knew instantly what I wanted to hear as we said our final goodbye to my beloved Alex: "How Can I Not Love You" by Joy Enriquez, my favourite song from one of my favourite films, *Anna and the King*. I also chose "Somewhere Over the Rainbow" by Eva Cassidy for exiting the church together, along with Josh Groban's "To Where You Are". I was too distressed to properly apply myself and select other music that resonated with me, and, to my regret, I did not include any of the songs that touched my heart, such as Nat

King Cole's "Unforgettable"; Andrea Bocelli and Celine Dion's "The Prayer"; Angelina Jordan's "Nothing Really Matters"; Katie Melua's "I Cried For You"; LeAnn Rimes' "How Do I Live?"; Coldplay's "Everglow"; and above all, "Look for me in Rainbows" by Vicki Brown, lyrics from which I have had inscribed on Alex's memorial stone. My favourite hymn, "Make Me a Channel of Your Peace", one the boys sang often at primary school, reminds me of when Alex was young. Tom chose a beautifully apt piece, "One Blood" by Terence Jay.

I knew that if I could get through my darling son's funeral, I could survive. However, I wanted to die, I should have died – I could not make it through the day. It seemed impossible, too horrendous for me to endure. Such thoughts consumed me as I awaited the arrival of the coffin carrying my boy and surrounded by flowers. As it reversed towards our driveway, I saw the floral arrangement I had chosen that spelled his name, A-L-E-X, in blue and yellow flowers. This made it too real, and the agony was beyond any words I know. I was robotic, functioning on the surface yet numb underneath, as though I was not really present. Well, perhaps I wasn't. I was in hell.

How proud Alex would have been of his brothers on that dreadful day. As Tom's choice of music played, my heart broke again for him and all that he would not experience with his big brother. When Paulo Nutini's "Growing Up Beside You" came on, my tears were for all three of my gorgeous sons and what would now never be. I still cannot listen to any of these beautiful songs because I am transported back in time to the pain of those moments as I said goodbye to Alex. When I heard "How Can I Not Love You" by Joy Enriquez during our final moments at the crematorium, I could not accept that he was edging further away from me forever. I cried out for him, repeating his name over and over and stretching my arm out to his coffin as it slipped away. Total and utter agony does not even come close: multiply that by infinity, and it would still not adequately describe the depth of my pain. I hope that one day I will be able to listen to this beautiful song again, but it just isn't possible for me yet...

Tom was both an emotional and physical support beside me throughout the day, and I have never loved him more or been prouder of him. My 20-year-old middle son had become my greatest strength and stood by me, whilst Steve kept a close eye on our lovely James as he said goodbye to the big brother he loved so much. My youngest son shed many tears that day for the first real time since we had heard of Alex's death, and my heart hurt for his loss at such an early age. It had been an obvious conclusion to me where the ashes should rest, but without telling a soul, I asked Tom to decide when and where the ashes should be scattered. After a few seconds' hesitation, he too said, "Alex's mountain in Canada on his birthday." Shortly thereafter, the flights were booked for the four of us to make that final, harrowing return journey in seven months' time.

The following is the eulogy Alex's stepdad wrote and delivered on the day I wish I had not lived to see:

The 14 July 1994 was a day of great joy. It saw the arrival of Alexander James into the world, and many of us here know that a baby was never more desperately awaited by a mother.

Alex was as bright as a button, cute, and blessed with a broad, beaming smile. I was lucky to witness Alex taking his first steps; he was gritty then as in later life, and he persevered to walk the full length of the room, to great applause and excitement.

Alex was a big brother to Thomas and in later years to James. A natural big brother, he doted on Thomas — and insisted on first rights to cuddle his new-born brother ahead of June, his grandmother. "My baby, Grandma. My baby, Grandma," he repeated to ensure the pecking order was well and truly understood, and I think Alex's pride and love for Tom is evident through the many photos shown earlier.

Alex greeted the news that Les was expecting a new arrival, James, with some concern and likely embarrassment. But, as soon as Alex held James in his arms, all his doubts melted away and he was smitten. James could do no wrong in Alex's eyes; James was the apple of his eye, and I know that being apart from James was so very hard for Alex.

Alex sailed through primary school and breezed through 11 GCSEs and 3 A levels — it has to be said, with little evidence of hard work or application. It was clear to all that Alex was bright with a gift — really, a gift – for the spoken and written word. Alex had places to study both law and English at Swansea and Northumbria Universities, places that he was destined not to take up, yet was more than capable of doing so.

Alex had a love of travel. He was 16 when he explored Rome. He insisted on doing this independently from the rest of the family, causing his mum much consternation. And he really did explore, navigating the Roman underground and the labyrinth of ancient streets and byways to seek out the heart of the city, its people, its history and, rather amusingly, the best pizza and gelato ice cream. Alex proudly guided us back to these pizza and gelato emporiums, and how right he was to have taken us.

He was 17 when he wrote of his adventures around Rome. It was a piece of work that Tarporley High School held out as "exemplar", and I quote here some extracts:

"… There were ancient Roman stone artefacts littered around like used coke cans… equally discarded and unvalued…"

"The new perfectly fuses with the traditional: terracotta roof tiles, sun-bleached walls and shutters… your ears are bombarded with high-pitched horns and two-stroke Vespa engines… this city is unique and provides a totally spellbinding experience that I will never forget."

How evocative, appreciative and insightful!

In between Alex's packed academic schedule – sorry Alex, forgive the wit, but I think you would smile at that one. In between Alex's packed academic schedule, he exploited a gap in the market and sold sweets at high school on, shall we say, the black market – doubling his money on every chocolate bar, can of drink and packet of sweets that he carefully chose for maximum appeal to less enterprising pupils. Inspired and generating a profit of over £1,000!

Alex loved all things to do with cars. At the age of five, he knew just about every make of car on the road. As a teenager, his knowledge of sports and supercars exceeded even mine. He was a dedicated keeper of a Top Gear Cool Wall, on which he and I assessed and classified motors as variously cool, sub-zero or plain boring.

But much, even all of this, you know. You and I saw Alex grow up as a child and teenager. What we didn't see so much was Alex as he grew from a teenager into a man, and this he did bravely, courageously, independently,

4,500 miles away on the west coast of Canada. Alex was but 18 years and 2 months old when he stepped onto those foreign shores. He had done his research well and immediately headed for a wonderfully beautiful mountain resort. Imagine brown bears by deep blue lakes, nestled within pine forests, giving rise to snow-capped mountains, and you will begin to see his new home. Alex started out with just the certainty of ten days accommodation booked in a hostel, but soon found work and started on his adventure.

I can still hear Alex selling the idea. "It's just for a year, Mum, really, just a year. I will return to take up my place at university."

Well, the one year turned into five years, and it became five years because Alex found himself in those faraway mountains and became part of a community, a family of young people who worked, lived, played and partied together.

Of course, there was also the attraction of on-tap, peak-to-peak snowboarding and skiing in winter months, and downhill mountain biking in the summer. But I think these were a sideshow; it was the warmth and courtesy of the Canadian people and the genuine and deep friendships that bound Alex to Canada and brought him happiness.

It is fair to say that we didn't appreciate the success Alex won in his place of work. Alex worked his way up through maintenance, poolside and bartending roles to become, at 21 years of age, the youngest to wait in their prestigious lounge bar. There, he worked alongside those in their late 20s, 30s and 40s, and he was even given responsibility of training new members of staff. Such was Alex's maturity. Alex pushed hard for this opportunity, often chiselling away at his boss for the chance, continually proving himself worthy in work, and expanding his knowledge through study courses covering food, wines and spirits.

Alex took great pride in his new home, and so enamoured was he that, one weekend, he telephoned home from beside a mountain lake. "Mum, I'm staying in Canada – I want to apply for permanent residency." This was, of course, heart-breaking news, but who could have denied him the chance of a life in that beautiful land so full of friendly, genuine people? In time, we know Alex would have become a Canadian citizen.

Thankfully, Les was able to overcome her fear of flying to make many trips to see Alex in Canada over the five years, both on her own and with Tom, James and me. These visits will be a trove of treasured memories, as will Alex's visits back to the UK and the overseas holiday he had with Les and James last year.

Alex saw more of the Americas than just his new hometown. He was at home around the seaboard city of Vancouver, and he also motored with friends down the west coast of America from San Francisco to Los Angeles, avidly taking in the sights, sounds and varying cultures.

But, I think, it is the words and stories of Alex's many friends in Canada that paint the best picture of the man Alex became. During the haunting days that Les and I spent in Canada just two weeks ago, so many of Alex's friends sought us out to share with us their thoughts and stories of Alex. This they did individually and then collectively, when some 60 of his friends met in his hotel to remember Alex with us.

So, let me share with you their words, thoughts and memories of Alex:

"Super-smart; the most intelligent guy I know. He knew more than the HR department about our residency applications, and he helped me to gain my visa."

"Courteous, impeccable manners, the ever-so-polite Brit; gracious."

"Reserved, shy – until you got to know the real Alex."

"Brave, so brave to adventure out here at only 18."

"Gentle, kind and respectful, Alex wouldn't hurt a fly."

"Intuitive, empathetic; Alex got other people."

"Gritty, determined – he challenged himself to perfect his work."

"Hard-working and respected, he was super focused. He didn't stop working when on duty. He was an absolute machine making drinks when bartending. He could remember monster orders and keep his cool when others would have panicked. He knew his trade; he would have gone far in the hospitality industry."

"A foodie and connoisseur of drinks – wow, could he talk about this flavour and that. He knew the best places to eat and knew all of the special offers. Then again, do you remember when he tried out being vegan? Alex had to share a cheese-less pizza. It must have been so awful, but I don't think the vegan thing lasted very long."

As an aside, I want to mention that Alex was fanatical about healthy eating, but never persuaded his Mum of the merits of dairy-free cakes. On one trip home from Canada, Alex baked a cake with a distinctly unusual and exotic list of ingredients. Lesley took one small bite of possibly the world's most expensive cake and pronounced, "Well Alex, that is the worst thing I have ever put in my mouth." Alex grinned that grin of his, shook his head but was undefeated and continued to expand his repertoire of new age recipes. That said, Alex did win us over with his amazing salads and healthy, tasty snacks – all produced with flair and panache. I also recall that Lesley was dubious about his bacon-wrapped salmon. He beamed as she reluctantly ate it. "Amazing," she said.

"Witty." It seems Alex had a store of apt, dry, witty one-liners; he often made his colleagues laugh with remarks about the hotels' more "difficult" guests. On one occasion, a few servers were complaining about not getting enough tips. Alex quipped sarcastically, "Well I'm sorry, there are some Tanzanian kids that have set up a 'Save the Lounge' fund for you guys this Christmas."

"Handsome, so handsome – if only he was older."

"Quirky: unbelievably, Alex took a watermelon to a cheese and wine evening. Ever since, someone has done the same and will do so to keep alive his memory. When Alex was invited to a camping weekend, he asked, 'What shall I bring?' The reply was, 'Oh, nothing,' so, guess what? Alex literally took nothing and ended up sleeping under the stars with borrowed clothes and coats as pillows and blankets."

"Often to be found having a beer with friends and a willing participant in several '12 pubs of Christmas' events."

"Always at a party or event," and when friends started to share photos, so very many showed Alex, happy and smiling.

A close friend wrote, "My biggest memories of Alex are his big grin and smile."

Alex was also described as:

Caring and unassuming: he quietly volunteered to help distribute coats for the poor in Vancouver on his day off, but he failed to mention this the following day when asked what he had done. "Oh, I just hung out," he said.

Alex was always more interested in others than himself. One of his work colleagues from the early days in housekeeping, a tall, strong man, was *visibly upset and said simply to me as he shook his head, "He always asked about my son, my boy, always."*

But, you know, the greatest of everything that was said to Les and me was how much his friends loved him. And they did, we saw that in their eyes, their tears and their desire to share with Lesley and me their stories of Alex. A friend wrote, "It was my pleasure today that I was chosen to serve the gathering for Alex's parents, work family and friends." For two of his closest female friends, he was their "baby brother." One of his best friends wrote "I just wish he could have known how much everyone loved and respected him."

Dear Alex, you entered this world and left this world much, much loved, and you leave all of us here today, and those of your extended family in Canada, so much poorer in your absence. But, most of all, immeasurably more, your mum adored you, will miss you and will always love you beyond the scope of mere words.

Many of Alex's friends in Canada were sad that they could not attend his funeral, but one of them sent me this after I had forwarded the eulogy to them:

"The eulogy was beautiful. I had tears streaming down my face the whole way through it, but it was good to hear so many stories about Alex's life in the UK. I really wish he could have known how many people adored him."

As I had uttered the first loving words to my beautiful new-born son, I also wanted to be the last person on earth to speak to him, and so I decided that, at the crematorium, it would be me who would say the final goodbye. I will never know how I managed this and only just spoke a few words about a mother's love for her cherished son before my grief overwhelmed me, but I had done it for Alex.

During those early days as news spread of Alex's tragic death, sympathy cards started to arrive, and they were a source of great comfort to me. I remember our lovely postman's face as I opened the door and he handed me another pile of cards, having delivered countless others the day before. He said, smiling, "Someone is popular," but horror spread across his face as he saw the agony on mine. I opened my mouth to say the dreadful words, "My son has died." He apologized, and I told him it was not his fault; he could not have known. I will not forget his genuine sorrow and kind words, and when he retired the following year, I gave him a retirement card with my thanks for his sensitivity and kindness.

For some reason that I cannot explain, rainbows have become significant to me when I need to feel Alex close by my side. There have been moments when both Steve and I have just looked at each other when we've seen a colourful arc in the sky, especially when I've felt sad or needed a sign that Alex is there. We have even named our new home Rainbows. When I was searching for the right words to put on Alex's memorial stone, I found a poem I liked called "Look for Me in Rainbows," and I adapted its ending with Alex's last words to me:

> *Time for me to go now, I won't say goodbye;*
> *Look for me in rainbows, way up in the sky.*
> *Every waking moment, and all your whole life through*
> *Just look for me and love me, as you know I loved you.*
>
> *Just wish me to be near you,*
> *And I'll be there with you.*
>
> *Love Always and Forever xxx*

Alex's stone rests beside a huge pine tree in a wooded area of our garden. It is next to a garden bench and is surrounded by a new wildflower area of the garden, which includes bluebells, primroses and poppies together with my favourite rose bushes, azaleas, rhododendrons and, of course, forget-me-nots – as if I need a flower to remind me of my beloved son. The area overlooks the Welsh mountains and is a beautiful place to sit and quietly contemplate memories of my boy. Our cat TC – Topcat, named after the cartoon series both Steve and I grew up watching in the 1960 and 70s – loves to sit next to this bench beside his catnip plant, keeping an eye on the resident squirrel high in the branches above. Alex was very fond of TC, and I am reminded of an occasion when he was last home. I went into his bedroom one morning to find 6-foot-2 Alex lying on the very edge of his double bed with TC sprawled out, claiming most of the space for himself – and Alex letting him! On the same visit home, Alex introduced TC to mouse games on YouTube, videos and animations designed to entertain cats. Why Alex thought to look for these, I can't imagine, but I remember us laughing at TC trying to catch the mice on the screen, and TC enjoys these games to this day. As I have mentioned before, Alex was a gentle and kind soul who would have harmed no one. How ironic that he unintentionally broke my heart.

The title of this chapter is "Letting Go Forever", yet I am still working on this. I need my darling Alex close to me for my very survival. The thought of letting go of him is the most difficult and painful of everything I have faced since that knock on the door changed my life forever. Robert Willis said, when talking about the death of his mum, English singer and presenter Cilla Black:

"You learn to accept the person you love is no longer there."

I cannot bear the darkness of visiting that place. I live like this so much of the time, holding Alex alive in my mind because I cannot bear the alternative. How will I ever let him go? Why should I? Books and people who supposedly are wiser than I on the subject of grief tell me that I have to let go, albeit in my own time. So far, after three years and six months, I can't. He is with me in my mind when I close my eyes, holding me, remaining close to me. What will happen to me if I let him go? He is my boy, my beloved son. I cannot… I am too scared to let him go. If I let him go, how can I breathe?

I accept that Alex is not coming back, and yet he is so real in my head that I can see him, chat to him, know what he would say and laugh at, agree or disagree with, and I can recall him in less than a second, although he is in my head virtually all the time anyway. He is with me, and I can only survive, it feels, by keeping him close to me.

Since Alex died, I have had to let go of a few close relatives and a close friend, although it is perhaps closer to the truth to say that it was their decision, not mine. Regardless, I mistakenly assumed that they would be there to support me, but for whatever reason, not everyone has the ability to be that person, and I have accepted this. The more I have walked with other parents through grief, the more I have heard of similar experiences. Kindness and love help immeasurably when faced with the darkest time in our lives. I believe that many can do a much better job at aiding those who are heartbroken by supporting them in their grief. I will never forget those who did and continue to do so. For those who did not, it seems that it is not a given, even though I had been their support when they needed it. Not everybody can show empathy and kindness. When I was already broken into a million pieces, letting go of those few was an extra sadness, but perhaps it is better to know who is incapable of being a loving support. This gave me a profound sense of sadness, yet strangely freedom, too, and was an unsurprising discovery.

"When the story of these times gets written,
we want it to say that we did all that we could,
and it was more than anyone could have imagined."
Edward de Bono

I have largely let go of pretending just to please others since Alex died. I have learnt that if I feel worse having seen someone and cannot resolve this, I am living in too much pain to continue doing so. It takes courage to let go of a relationship that no longer works, but when you are broken down to your rawest self, it is essential in order to heal. When your heart is shattered, you cannot cope with any additional pain.

Letting go of the thought that I could have controlled the dreadful outcome of his death is an ongoing effort. It may take my lifetime to really forgive myself for not keeping Alex alive, for not knowing that he was suffering, as he chose not to tell me. Some days I still berate myself and think I could have, should have saved him. It has taken me over three years but, together with counselling during the first year and especially with Steve and Tom's continuing help, I am beginning to accept that I did not have the power to keep Alex alive. I have had to give Alex ownership in his decision to end his life. I did not and perhaps could not make the outcome different. Letting go of the notion that I could and can influence my boys' lives has not been an easy journey. Their paths are their own, as are the choices – and the mistakes – they make along the way. Despite Alex's letters he left for us, only he really knew the depth of his pain and why he felt it was impossible for him to continue living.

I have not yet found solace in religion, but I respect that a faith can provide immense comfort for the bereaved. I have been asked whether I have rediscovered the faith I felt more keenly when Alex and Tom were young. I have not found comfort in religion thus far, although I respect people of any and all beliefs. However, I am open to the thought that I might have been given the strength I need to face this tragedy by a higher presence. For me, awful, random things happen to good people, and it is so very hard to fathom why a loving, protective God cannot spare their suffering. I do, however, understand that it is not the will of God, if indeed there is one, to make human beings feel such pain. Alex was such a kind, gentle and generous soul, and I wanted to believe that there was a God who would be watching over him. The fact that he returned home in a coffin has not helped secure any religious belief, and so my thoughts on the subject are complicated and unresolved. It is more important to me to feel that my darling son is now at peace. My boys have made up their own minds about religion and thus far have chosen not to embrace it, although we can't say what Alex has experienced, if anything, since his death.

I do believe, however, that there is something more beyond our earthly existence, something spiritual that is bigger than ourselves, and I want to believe that one day Alex and I will be reunited. I want to believe that the strength I have found to survive this has come from above... I recently heard the beautiful song "Jealous of the Angels", sung by Katherine Jenkins, and the heartfelt words reflect what I want to believe in: the hope that my darling Alex is now in heaven or wherever it is that is beautiful, safe and eternally peaceful. None of us on earth knows for sure what exists and what does not, but we can hope. It is only when we leave this world that we find out. I feel that Alex took a piece of my heart to wherever the onward journey leads to, and I will never get it back, as it belongs to him. I have had to find light in the darkness, a whisper of hope that I will find peace, and perhaps something greater than us is guiding me.

Agonizingly, the time came to face letting go of everything that had been Alex, letting go of his ashes, his earthly remains. As I type those words, over three years later, I am quietly sobbing as the pain inside me is overwhelming. There was only one place on earth that Tom and I could choose to scatter our precious Alex's ashes: his favourite mountain in Canada. And we also agreed that we had to do this on Alex's birthday. So, Steve, Tom, James and I returned to Canada seven months after Alex's death to spread his ashes on what would have been his 24th birthday, on top of the mountain where he lived and had spent so many happy hours skiing. Tom and I just knew that this was what Alex would have chosen. I believe that my beloved son is now free of pain and at eternal peace. These beautiful mountains captured his soul, and his final resting place sits amongst the wildflowers growing freely in springtime and is blanketed in snow that glistens like diamonds in the winter sunshine.

"If I can stop one heart from breaking,
I shall not live in vain;
If I can ease one life the aching,
Or cool one pain,
Or help one fainting robin
Unto his nest again,
I shall not live in vain."

Emily Dickinson

CHAPTER 7

ALEX'S LEGACY

Alex was intelligent and an eloquent writer, and his own harrowing words, which are being used to help other men, can be found at the end of this chapter. My precious son hauntingly described how he had "become merely an empty shell yearning to feel human and alive but physically unable, trapped like a refugee within my own body." Alex concluded his final letter to me by asking me to share his suffering in the hope of helping others and wrote:

"We stand on the shoulders of those who came before."

That was typical of my kind, sensitive son. If there was suffering, Alex cared. Especially if it was children or young people facing hardship, illness or pain. After Alex died, we visited a children's hospice in Canada and made a donation in his memory. I asked that the donation be used to take severely disabled children with life-limiting illnesses to be sleigh-skied down the mountain near to where Alex lived and where he spent many happy times skiing with his friends. I know that Alex would have been humbled that, in his memory, these kids enjoyed the fun, magic and freedom of adapted skiing so that they, too, could create lasting memories for themselves and their families.

Alex lived his life to the fullest doing the things he loved, especially so in his years living in Canada. He was mesmerized by the beauty of the mountains and wilderness all around him. He was a good and loyal friend, and for someone so young, he showed such maturity and wisdom. Alex had a thirst for knowledge and showed kindness, empathy and compassion to those less fortunate. He always maintained a keen sense of humour and often charmed people with his smile that could light up the room. Alex's story is not just about his tragic and untimely death, but also about his life.

In the early days and weeks following Alex's death, I thought about setting up a foundation in his name to help those suffering from similar devastating effects of circumcision. I have since learnt how desperately affected many men are across the globe, across different races and religions, and sadly how others have also chosen to end their lives as a result. However, I decided that others better equipped than myself were already doing this and so to publicize Alex's story would better honour his last request of me. Early on in my research of how to achieve this, I came across a UK-based charity, 15 Square, whose mission is to help men suffering from the effects of circumcision. I contacted them and learnt that, sadly, Alex's case was far from unique. Since then, I have given talks and online presentations on behalf of the charity, and I was humbled to be recently appointed as their ambassador.

David Smith, the charity's chief officer, is one of an ever-growing number of academics from various disciplines who want to see circumcision used as a last resort. I have learnt that there are alternatives to circumcision, which are often effective and non-invasive. The charity seeks to promote this whilst holding authorities to account and providing a voice for those affected, whether that be physically or psychologically, or more often, both. For some, circumcision has few adverse effects, and it is a routine procedure, but for others it is not, and there needs to be research into the frequency with which the disturbing consequences arise. It is time for health professionals to listen to the evidence and the suffering of these men and not to dismiss them as either a tiny minority or as suffering from psychological issues. In many cases, including Alex's, it is not mental health that is the problem in the first place, although their physical suffering may well adversely affect their state of mind. I also feel strongly that there needs to be research on the link between circumcision and suicide because, sadly, I know there is one.

Many men from all over the world have contacted the charity as a direct result of the publicity of Alex's story. This made me realize that by helping others, I was also helping myself. I was pleased to be asked to be the guest speaker at the annual general meeting of the charity, and the resulting standing ovation – with many of the audience in tears – was a standout moment that will live with me forever. I felt Alex so closely by my side in that room as I delivered my speech and knew that he would be proud.

The following is a statement from David Smith that I am pleased to include in this chapter:

Alex was a normal, healthy young man who, following his circumcision in adulthood, suffered so greatly that he was driven to take his own life in 2017. Alex is not alone in having suffered this fate but, such is the taboo nature of circumcision, that these tragedies have not been widely reported. Alex is, however, unique in my experience because he left behind the legacy of an eloquent account of his suffering, and his final wish was that his message should be heard.

I first met Lesley in 2018 when Caroline Lowbridge, a BBC journalist, was working on a television feature about male circumcision. I was providing information on behalf of 15 Square, a charity that helps men who have been damaged either physically or psychologically through circumcision and seeks to promote non-surgical alternatives for phimosis. Lesley gave so moving an account of Alex's story – and her suffering as the surviving mother – that the day the interview went on air, 15 Square was swamped with enquiries from men equally distressed by their circumcisions. It changed the direction of the charity and has continued to do so as more men read or hear of Alex's story.

Lesley's work to date in publicizing Alex's story will surely have surpassed his expectations. After her appearance on the BBC, Lesley has gone on to give interviews to the British national press and, as ambassador for 15 Square, has reached out to a global audience through social media.

I believe that Alex would be proud that his words are promoting change and helping men understand that their suffering is not unique. In helping fellow sufferers feel less alone, I know that Alex has saved many men from suicide. Alex's words have made a difference and will continue to make a difference, and I wish I could have met him to say thank you. His legacy will live on...

In addition, the following words have kindly been written by Jason Metters, project manager for 15 Square:

Alex's story is both heart-breaking and inspiring. On the one hand, he had an internal battle trying to come to terms with the impacts that a circumcision had on his life, and on the other hand, there is a clear message within the letter that he left behind: tell the others! He spent his final words earnestly trying to deter others from walking the same difficult path that he endured.

I first became involved with the charity 15 Square in 2016 after hearing about the trauma that many men suffer after receiving a circumcision. It was a shock at first, but also made absolute sense. One of the most sensitive parts of the body is bound to have significance to many men. After reading hundreds of personal accounts shared with the charity, I know only too well that circumcision can leave pain, discomfort and changes in sensitivity in its wake. In Alex's case he was not warned of these problems as doctors are often all too eager to downplay the significance of the procedure. There needs to be fully informed consent. Circumcision should come with a warning label, and Lesley Roberts has given us that label by sharing Alex's words. Withholding information on potential side effects can have dire consequences.

What is significant about Alex is that he wanted his story to be made public after his tragic death. Rather than hiding his trauma, which is often natural for such a private issue, Alex wanted to prevent further suffering at the expense of his own privacy. He bravely expressed exactly what his situation was in specific detail and left no uncertainty as to the origin of his pain. His story should be heard by parents, doctors, politicians and men worldwide so that they can have a window into the thought processes that are behind circumcision grief and act accordingly.

I hope that Alex's story encourages other men who are struggling to share their experiences and to seek help before they are overwhelmed. I am enormously grateful that Alex was bold enough to step up and express himself before he left us. The fact that he did shows his caring nature and his desire to save others from his fate.

During the first year following Alex's death, several family members questioned the wisdom of writing about Alex and dedicating my time to suicide prevention and publicizing the risks of circumcision. They thought that this would only serve to prolong my grief. While I understand they had my best interest at heart, I would say that, unless you have lost a child, you cannot know what helps, and it is for the bereaved parent – and them alone – to know how best to handle the horror of their child's death. Apart from carrying out Alex's last wishes to publicize his story to help other young men, I am committed to suicide prevention. If I can save one other young person from ending their life when it is only just beginning, or save one other mum's heart from being broken, then I will feel that I have achieved something important. As I have said before, there is no moving on, only moving forward. It is also important to me to keep Alex's memory alive, and in sharing my wonderful boy and his suffering with the world, I feel that I am honouring him, as he will not be forgotten, and his untimely death will not have been in vain.

Prior to Alex's suicide, I naively thought people chose circumcision either because of religious beliefs, usually carried out on infants, or perhaps that it was a routine procedure for those who had a medical issue and for whom there was no alternative. I have subsequently learnt so much more, yet I am by no means an expert on the subject, and I have no medical background. I have talked to several urologists and doctors to gain their perspective on this operation and to understand the incidence of success and failure. To date, it has been my experience that the medical profession, in general, perceive circumcision as a routine procedure with very minimal risk of adverse side effects. I now know from my own experience that this operation can be anything but routine, and that it can have lasting, devastating consequences. I am deeply uncomfortable with the general view, and I have tried to understand more through research and by talking or corresponding with others who have been adversely affected by circumcision. I am also learning from medical experts around the world who are seeking to promote change in how we view the procedure. It is heartening that there are medical experts who share similar concerns about circumcision and who have been interested in reading Alex's tragic account.

I would like Alex's death to provoke more discussion about the potential problems of circumcision and, ultimately, help bring about proper disclosure of potential adverse side effects as part of the consent-to-surgery process. Tragically, Alex was not alone in suffering pain and dysfunction following circumcision, nor was he alone in taking his own life as a direct result.

Of course, there is a great deal of stigma attached to this sensitive subject, with sensitivity amplified by its connection to religious rites. I do not seek to malign any religious group, being respectful of all religions and atheism. Alex was brought up to view religion as an individual's choice, a human right, and his and my desire to publicize his suffering is based solely on humanity and without reference to any religious group.

Several men have written to me as a result of reading of Alex's suicide on BBC news online, in magazines or on social media. I am beyond grateful for such letters, and I am so proud that Alex's story is helping others. I reproduce below one letter:

Dear Lesley,

I read the BBC piece about your son Alex last night, and it touched my heart – so much so that I woke at 3am thinking about it and resolved to write to you.

Your son clearly had a beautiful character and was also sensitive, strong and honest in understanding and expressing what had been done to him.

It cannot have been easy for you to go public against a background of such enormous personal loss. However, the fact that you have honoured his wishes by carrying forward his message is truly admirable and demonstrates great personal strength.

I'm sure there are thousands of circumcised men who will read the piece, relate to it and yet do or say nothing. However, on their behalf as well as mine, I want you to know that Alex's voice has not gone unheard. Hopefully, his message, carried through you, will help to bring an end to unnecessary circumcision.

You've done a wonderful thing,
With warmth and best wishes,
P.

Thank you, P. It helps to know that Alex's suffering and death has not been in vain.

Alex had so much to give to the world. He will always be so much more than his death, and the loss is profound and life changing. It is too late to save my precious son, but I hope his story can bring awareness to the risks associated with circumcision, remind people that they have alternatives to this surgery, and above all, highlight the need for suicide prevention.

> *"The things you do for yourself are gone when you are gone, but the things you do for others remain as your legacy."*
> *Kalu Kalu*

Alex touched and left his mark on so many with his kindness, sharp wit, intellect, eloquence and good humour. Alex is remembered fondly by so many in Canada, and it is such a comfort to me that he made such a positive impact. A smile came easily to Alex, and I will never forget his lovely smile. It is incredibly powerful to smile, despite crying inside, and I try to smile at familiar faces on my daily walks by the sea.

I am reminded of the words I recently read of Joe Kennedy, Sr., who outlived three of his four sons and a daughter:

> *"When one of your loved ones goes out of your life, you think what he might have done with a few more years. And you wonder what you are going to do with the rest of yours. Then one day, because there is a world to be lived in, you find yourself part of it, trying to accomplish something – something he did not have time enough to do. And perhaps that is the reason for it all. I hope so."*

Alex's presence remains in the endless love Tom, James and I carry within us. He did not pass through this life unnoticed, and he inspired so many with his humour, kindness, empathy courage and compassion. The beautiful smile mentioned by many of his friends that could light up a room will be remembered.

This book is Alex's legacy and I include his own words below which are far more powerful and eloquent than mine as they explain the reason that Alex chose to end his life; his words deserve to be heard and I hope the world will listen. Alex's written words have already made a difference to many men around the globe. I could not be prouder. I failed to protect my dear son from death, but I can spend the rest of my life protecting him from being forgotten.

— ~ —

To Whom It May Concern,

The following is information that I wish to share to provide an account of my personal experience of circumcision. I hope it may raise awareness in parents considering this for their children and inform adults finding themselves in a similar situation. If my experience can benefit anyone, then my opinions will have served their purpose. We stand on the shoulders of those who came before us.

For several years, I suffered with a tight foreskin. I did not perceive it as a true medical issue until I researched and discovered the diagnosis, phimosis, that was responsible for the symptoms I was experiencing. I consulted a doctor who suggested stretching the foreskin and using a steroid cream. I was under the false impression that the cream alone would facilitate the stretching. I was poorly instructed on how to do this. I was previously unaware of these stretching techniques and that the use of expander rings was also necessary for it to be effective.

A few weeks later, I went back to the doctor in the belief that the stretching was not working. He suggested a circumcision. I believe that he demonstrated the common medical misconception that a full circumcision for phimosis is best practice. My research into the alternative treatments other than circumcision and the potential consequences of the operation were insufficiently comprehensive.

I had partially accepted the doctor's view about the procedure. The research I did was using a small smartphone, my only digital device for internet browsing at the time. These searches revealed little detailed information. I briefly attempted investigating the topic on a public computer, but the nature of relevant websites and the associated imagery made me uncomfortable in the public setting, so I stopped. I came to trust the opinions of the doctor. I did not think that extensive research into the procedure and its consequences should be necessary prior to undergoing any such surgery.

I did enquire more of the surgeon about stretching and less destructive procedures such as preputioplasty, which preserves the healthy foreskin and its function, but was met with a very negative response. I was trusting of his authoritative opinion in my desperation to resolve the issue of a tight foreskin. I did not appreciate then that skin expansion may well have succeeded if performed correctly. Retrospectively, I believe that the doctor did not discuss in sufficient depth all other possible treatment options that may have been available to me or described in enough detail the negative consequences of circumcision that can occur. Had I been given such information, I may have chosen a different option to full surgical circumcision. At least I would have been able to have considered this information and come to a balanced, reflective decision. I feel that I went into this surgery with insufficient information. If I had participated in a proper process of fully informed consent, which I do not believe I did, I may have opted for other treatments. If I had then chosen surgical circumcision, at least I would have been aware of the potential problems that can occur afterwards. I do not feel I was given this opportunity. A combination of trust in the authority of doctors, euphemistic terminology, desperation to resolve a tight foreskin and poor information pushed me to accept the circumcision. I now regard this as an extreme solution.

I felt the topic was taboo and not appropriate to discuss with others around me. This may be due to individual factors within myself and my introverted personality, but I believe it is also due to societal factors about such subjects. I think that the negative effects of circumcision from which some men suffer are not well recognized. These men are largely misunderstood by society and also by many medical professionals.

As someone who has suffered the negative effects of circumcision and who regrets having it done, I know exactly what these feelings and experiences are. I have been left in a permanent state of chastity, tension and emotional imbalance. The realities of this are horrific. I believe this topic must be discussed with more honesty, medical accuracy and full acknowledgment of all effects caused by circumcision. All potential patients should routinely participate in detailed fully informed consent before any such surgery. There must be adequate information given and resources provided to allow one to make decisions that they can live with afterwards, should they be unfortunate enough to suffer a poor outcome.

Within days of the circumcision, I began to have serious regrets. The doubts I had beforehand that were silenced by the doctor's advice had unfortunately become true. Nature knows best – how can removing a section of healthy tissue improve upon nature's evolved design? Certain doubts concerned me prior to surgery, and yet I still consented to it, which demonstrates that information from multiple sources that circumcision is a correct and a beneficial treatment for a phimosis is not always the case. Other options should have been discussed with me in detail, and more information should have been more readily available.

The consequential physical effects I have suffered from circumcision have proved jarring. I constantly experience an agonizing stimulation of the glans and frenulum area from my clothing, which has not subsided significantly over time. I liken this to the experience that one would suffer from if one's eye would be subject to removal of its eyelid.

Wishing for desensitization to develop for a reduction to this constant low-level stimulation ultimately means less desired sensitivity when it is needed. Doctors informed me that the glans would function successfully without the foreskin. In reality this is not true. The Meissner's corpuscles and other erotogenic nerve endings present within the foreskin and frenulum are responsible for sexual reflexes that cannot be triggered from the glans alone. The foreskin also has a secondary function of protecting the glans and keeping it moist. Once removed the glans becomes dry, keratinized and significantly decreased in sensitivity.

I have also experienced two years of uncomfortable sensations from the scar in the area of my frenulum and erectile dysfunction – all of this is despite being told to expect a maximum six-month recovery. Where I once had a sexual organ, I have now been left with a numb stick. This is a nightmare predicament. My sexuality has been left in tatters. It has proved torturous to me and has given me insomnia. Although difficult to quantify, I would suggest that I have been stripped of 75 per cent of the sensitivity in my penis. The pleasure my body should provide is all but gone, instead replaced with permanent discomfort and subsequent angst. Whole body orgasms have become a distant memory, a now unattainable state. A huge amount of passion has been removed from my life. It has fundamentally changed the person I am in a host of negative ways.

The lack of knowledge and respect for the functions of the foreskin and other tissue removed in circumcision is a widespread concern and not appreciated enough by the medical profession. Circumcision should not be regarded as a minor procedure that removes a piece of unnecessary tissue, but as a destructive procedure that can have very negative physical and emotional consequences.

I was a consenting adult at the time of the procedure and, therefore, substantial responsibility lies with myself. However, it must not be overlooked that this procedure was advocated by medical professionals.

Since my circumcision, I have become aware of the lucrative industry surrounding this procedure. In addition, as someone who is totally in favour of gender equality, I believe that circumcision should be considered in the same way as that of female genital mutilation, which is rightly widely deplored.

Prior to the surgery I had enquired with the doctor whether sensitivity would be lost. He assured that, in his experience, there was no loss in sensitivity. I found this unrealistic even before I understood the true level of the loss of pleasurable sensation that there ultimately was. This was another example of misguided information that haunts me daily. The phrase "trust your instincts" regrettably resonates with me.

Every year, millions of males that are circumcised are robbed of the fundamental, primitive experiences intended by nature. Childhood victims of circumcision will tragically never be able to fully comprehend what has been taken from them. Unnecessary circumcision, I feel, is a vicious circle of violence that must be halted. It is a travesty that this practice continues in the 21st century.

The combined physical and emotional discomfort of circumcision has transformed my life into one where internal peace is absent. Maintaining dignity and composure has proved difficult. It has become ever increasingly apparent how extensive the damage to my body has been and the impact this has had on my life. The physical discomfort is so prominent that it is always at the forefront of my mind. The severity of the daily physical sensations that bombard my body are difficult to put into words. Intact genitals are a human right. I have found it surreal and crushing that I was, for a short period, ashamedly convinced to deny this to myself. My experiences have motivated me to share the message to conserve this fundamental human right for others; the removal of healthy bodily tissue should never be promoted.

I have sought professional psychological therapy including from sexual health professors, but the damage caused by surgery has proved too enormous for any emotional support to rectify. Science has not yet advanced to enable the regrowth or replacement of such removed tissue and restoration of its function. There is no true medical solution for these issues. The consequences have cast a dark shadow on my life. I once lived in colour, but now I exist in monochrome. No therapy has alleviated this shadow because it cannot address the physical symptoms at the root cause of the issue. I had challenges in my life prior to this surgery, like all human beings.

The fallout from circumcision has gradually constricted the life out of my soul. I have become an empty shell, yearning to feel human and alive but physically unable, trapped as a refugee within my own body.

Emotionally, I am unable to live in internal peace or human dignity. I will be in a state of peace at the time of publishing this. I wish flourishment to all those who read this. For any distress caused to others because of my death, I am remorseful, as it is not my intention to inflict any suffering. Hopefully, progression will be achieved in medicine and society to prevent and eradicate this unnecessary and inhumane mutilation from being inflicted on others in future.

My final wish would be for my organs to be donated if and where possible (perhaps not the penis!) – I am a registered transplant donor.

Alexander James Hardy (2017)

"Love is eternal; the aspect may change but not the essence."

Vincent Van Gogh

CHAPTER 8

THE AGONY OF SUICIDE

Suicide is one of the most wounding of human experiences and has become a worldwide epidemic. While it does not discriminate between age, class, gender or religion, the incidence of suicide by young men dominates the statistics. Death by suicide leaves unanswered questions, heartbreak, and often complicated grief for those left behind. I know that it will be my life's work to rediscover my own internal peace.

Alex's despair brought him to a dark place. As he described in his last emails, his chronic, constant pain changed him, and he began to withdraw into himself. I believe that he showed some subtle signs of disconnection, yet was clever enough to hide this from almost everyone. I remember clearly discussing my concerns with a close friend who, upon hearing of Alex's death, gently said to me, "You knew." She had listened when I had expressed my unease, the feeling telling me that something was wrong. With all my heart, I wish I had listened to my instincts.

I have since read about the psychological term "disenfranchised", which is used to describe someone who feels alone with their pain, isolated, desperate and unable to be reached emotionally. When Alex and I had loving telephone conversations towards the end of his life, I again felt unease, yet he was extremely careful not to arouse any concerns. The unrelenting pain wore him down, and life became overwhelming – and this was when suicide became an option.

It was only when I heard of Alex's death that I discovered the enormity of his suffering and how this had led him to decide that it outweighed the potential for a happy life. In our last conversation a week before he died, I asked Alex how he really was and told him how excited I was to visit him the following week. Alex chatted for an hour, saying he was fine and spoke of his resilience, trying to reassure me that all was well. It pains me to know now that my dear, wonderful, caring, dignified and thoughtful boy was masking his pain and lying to me to spare my worries. He had become convinced that I could not help him, and so he chose not to share his struggles with me. How I wish he had. Alex had probably already decided to end his suffering and his life.

It has been excruciatingly difficult for me to accept, but I have had to understand that because I was not living in Alex's shoes, I can never truly know how he felt, as he alone knew how impossible it had become for him. My son's heartbreakingly eloquent suicide letters did provide many answers, and this was typical of his love for us. He tried to make it easier on us by explaining what he felt unable to say during his lifetime. Of course, Alex could never lessen our pain, but we are grateful to him that he left us his last, loving words, which we treasure.

The horror of Alex's last moments haunts me, especially as I try to close my eyes at night. I discovered that, on his last evening, Alex had been to his local bar and seen friendly faces. What had he been thinking on his way home? Had he cried, despite his bravery? Was he afraid, despite his resolve? Did he say, as I suspect, "I'm sorry, Mum," knowing how his death was going to break my heart? I know that his last thoughts would have been for me, Tom and James. I have since learnt that my precious boy would have lapsed into unconsciousness within seconds.

Suicide compounds the anguish of a more "normal" death. It is different, as it brings with it not only the normal grief of death, but additionally the extra agonies of guilt, confusion and limitless questions that will never be adequately answered. We experience excruciating heartache, incomprehensible to those who have not been bereaved by suicide. Perhaps the worst part is the shock, and even now as I write this looking out at the beautiful Welsh mountains, I can barely believe the words I am thinking and writing and that they relate to Alex. His death has become part of me and is at the forefront of my mind day and night, and I cannot yet imagine a time when it or he will not be.

Suicide has become an unwelcome yet permanent part of the lives of my family, and I am especially saddened that this is now a part of Alex's brothers' back stories. I hope that, with the passage of time, it will not be at the forefront of who they are, and I can say with quiet optimism that their brother's death does not always dominate their thoughts.

I read somewhere that suicide is not for "sissies". It certainly requires enormous strength and courage for those who have no choice but to face the rest of their lives knowing that their loved one chose to end their own. To die by suicide is generally not considered a crime, but in my darkest hours, I have thought perhaps it should be, as it creates such misery, guilt and untold agony in those left behind. It sadly transfers the pain to someone else and is not something you can expect to ever get over. Instead, you learn to live alongside it.

In the weeks that followed Alex's death, I was sickened to discover suicide websites, some even encouraging the act, and many promoting the best means to do so. It is an outrage that such pages exist, and I feel they are the dark side of the online world. So many vulnerable, often young people are enticed by such sites to end their lives. The fact that such harmful content is available at the touch of a button surely requires stricter legislation, or even needs to be made illegal, if we are to tackle the tragically increasing number of young people who die this way.

What would I say to other young men or, indeed, anyone contemplating ending their life, is that life is precious, and suicide is never the answer. It is also the most intense loss imaginable for those left behind. You will not be good at everything, but there will be something in which you excel – seek to find this. Alex did find his passion, and it brought him much happiness, but the pain left after his circumcision became too much for him to bear. Perhaps if he had shared his suffering, more could have been done to help him. He was much loved. To anyone else feeling desperate, call someone. Anyone.

Tell them what's wrong. Do not end your life. You matter too much. Suicide is often the result of irrational thinking caused by depression. This is so difficult for me to process, as Alex was such a logical thinker – perhaps too black and white – but resilient, which is a word he used to describe himself. Alex had no history of depression, and although he left us with letters explaining the decision to end his life, not all questions arising from his death are satisfactorily answered. There will always be a why. Suicide is a terrifying, permanent and utterly tragic response to extreme pain. Experts tell us that it is rarely one single reason that leads a person to complete this act. We know from Alex's letters that he had decided to end his life because of the debilitating effects of a circumcision he had undergone two years earlier, and this overwhelmed his ability or desire to continue living. We do not know when he made the decision to kill himself.

The suicide of a loved one irrevocably changes us, and our world never returns to its previous existence. There is no escape, as the reality is never going to change, the narrative is set in stone forever. It's a perpetual cycle of pain – a never-ending nightmare. Others will recognize these emotions from difficult situations they may have faced in their lives, but the grief of losing a child is like no other experience. It's as close to hell as it gets. Believe me, not for the first time in writing this book, I wish with all my heart that I were not qualified to know this.

Those left to grieve a suicide remember every act of kindness, however seemingly insignificant, when their whole world implodes, tearing their heart into a million fragments, never again to be reassembled in its previous form. The opposite is also true, meaning unkindness, whether intentional or not, is an unwelcome visitor to someone who's already shattered. Every parent who has lost a child to suicide, and indeed every parent of a deceased child, will likely experience human nature at its best and worst: the compassion and kindness of some, and the social freezing-out from others. I have certainly experienced both. Of course, there are occasions when perceived rejection may be the result of the other person's uncertainty of what to say to the bereaved, but sometimes their disappearance is sadly intentional. If you do not know what is appropriate or helpful to say, don't worry – you cannot make it any worse than it already is.

I am grateful to have Alex's brothers, who want desperately for me to feel joy again. My love for them is my reason to seek it, as Alex asked of me. However, I know that there is no fixing a broken heart. Survivors of a child's suicide face the ongoing daily challenge of survival. Life becomes an entirely different landscape. I often contemplate that if Alex had known the depth of agony his death would cause – and it is astounding to me that he did not – he may not have taken his own life. However, I have to accept that Alex's suffering had become untenable for him. Those that knew and loved him, especially his many lovely friends in Canada, described Alex as a kind and gentle soul who would not intentionally hurt anyone, least of all his brothers and me. I truly believe that my boy was in such agony that he lost sight of what his death would do to those closest to him. Help was available to Alex, he was so loved, and he mattered to so many of us, and yet he did not ask. Had he said anything, there would have been no judgement, no shame – only care and compassion. Perhaps this is why I have never felt angry with him. I feel only desperate sadness at learning of his suffering and that he did not share it with anyone. Life is precious and worth living, and suicide is never the answer.

As I try to pick up the pieces of my life, I am plagued by nightmares in which Alex is calling for me because he needs me, and I am not there. Sometimes, it feels like he is drowning, and I can't save him. It is an overwhelming pain, and I have to control myself from becoming hysterical with grief, desperate to scream at him, to anyone, to just bring my boy back and make this horror not be true. I feel guilt for the things I got wrong and sadness for the things I got right but can never do again. I feel desperate that I did not save Alex, yet I have to accept that I am not responsible for his death. The only person responsible for Alex's suicide was Alex, but it has perhaps been easier to take that responsibility upon myself, and this is destructive. I believe that anyone who dies by suicide does not deserve blame, as they were gripped by despair and a loss of hope. I do know for certain that my gentle son did not fully appreciate the devastating impact of his suicide. I would have done anything to help my precious son and would give anything to have Alex back, if even for a minute, even to say goodbye, but, of course, I would never be able to let him go. I almost battle with myself, forcing myself to accept the most heart-wrenching thing in all of this: Alex is not coming back, ever. But he now lives in me, remains part of me, and I will never let him go. My love for him is infinite and did not die when his heart stopped.

It is impossible not to feel that another tragedy awaits me. My life was once normal, unremarkable, but now it feels anything but, and for all the wrong reasons. I gave my boys the wings to fly, and both Alex and Tom grew to be confident young adults keen to explore the world. It is especially frightening for me now, as Tom works in New Zealand on the other side of the world from me, but I have had to let him go, as I did Alex. I have to remember that it is not my job or my right to hold my boys back, although it is now an almighty struggle to tell myself that Tom and James will be safe when nothing seems safe anymore.

It goes with the awful territory of losing a child by suicide that the guilt it leaves behind is painful terrain to traverse. Counselling and the support from both Tom and Steve have helped me to learn to be compassionate with myself and see that I did the best with the knowledge I had. James, too, has played his part in helping me begin to heal. Being so young when his big brother died, he has needed me to continue to function as his mum in the way I always did, thereby providing a focus in my everyday life. Tom reassures me when I doubt that Alex knew how much I loved him. I know this to be true, but it's such loving confirmation when Tom comforts me and prevents me from falling into the abyss of guilt that helps no one. I know that Alex, who said as much in his last email to me, reassured me of this, too.

In navigating my way through the pain left by Alex's suicide, I knew after a few months that I needed professional bereavement support, yet group therapy was not for me. As in all professions, there are good and bad counsellors. After having a few poor appointments, which I finished after less than ten minutes – you just intuitively know – I found a wonderful counsellor who provided a safe place for me to expose my pain and help me process Alex's death. There was a strangely reassuring coincidence when I entered the room for my first counselling session. There on the wall were several prints of Winnie the Pooh. Shortly after Alex's death, I had bought a framed print of Winnie the Pooh, as it summed up what I needed to believe. I still read the words under the picture most days, as it calms me when I am desperate for Alex not to be gone forever:

> If ever there is a tomorrow
> when we're not together…
> there is something
> you must always remember.
>
> You are braver than you believe,
> stronger than you seem,
> and smarter than you think.
>
> But the most important thing is,
> even if we're apart…
> I'll always be with you.

There will always be so many thoughts of "if only…" for the loved ones of a person who dies by suicide. The questions and guilt will take me a lifetime to process and forever cause me to feel that I could have done something to save my cherished son. Looking back, I tried to ask my darling boy on our last holiday together if anything was troubling him. It was just a feeling, a mother's instinct that I could not really articulate. It was a faint, almost subconscious yet recurring terror, gnawing at my insides. I mentioned my deepest fears to my husband, a close relative and a close friend, but I convinced nobody that there could be tragedy lying in wait and, truthfully, I did not even believe it myself. As I even write these words, I cannot do justice in writing a description of those feelings, apart from to say it was just a fear, an instinct, perhaps so horrifying to me that I did not want to or could not face it. When I did try and ask Alex about any worries he might have, I was *almost* accepting of his total denials that anything was wrong. This can evolve into psychological torture, as survivors ask themselves repeatedly the very questions any of us would ask: *What could I have done differently? What signs did I miss? How could I have not known the depths of his despair? How could he have left me?* How I wish I had listened more carefully to myself. The harsh fact remains, Alex did not choose to share his pain with me.

The word suicide conjures horror, yet even this is an inadequate description of the depth of pain when your beloved child chooses to end their life. Nobody knows when tragedy might strike, and I have no words to adequately describe such agony, the never-ending yearning for a cherished child. The permanence of my new situation is not going to alter, and irrespective of how much I yearn for it to be different, it never will be. I try and convince myself that Alex is only a heartbeat away, and he is waiting for me. This brings me comfort in the interminably long, dark hours of the night.

Alex's suicide has brought me to the darkest of places, and there have been brief moments when I could have succumbed to choosing death over life. At times it felt like if I was dead, then the pain would stop, and I would hopefully be reunited with my beloved son. However, I could never inflict such pain upon my other lovely sons. I understand that to have such thoughts after losing your child to suicide, or losing a child in any circumstances, could lead you down that destructive path. However, it is important to acknowledge this eternal yearning can be accommodated within your new life. Suicide leaves only devastation and agony in its wake, and, most especially if you are a parent, it is never the answer. I would urge anybody contemplating ending their life to reach out to someone, anyone, and to recognize that their life matters hugely, and they are of value. Alex was adored, cherished and so much loved, yet I think in talking to no one, he tragically lost all perspective and hope.

Suicide encourages the parent left behind to feel that they failed in the most basic parenting skill, and this is not helped by the lack of support offered to those left behind. I failed to keep my child alive.

Several friends, neighbours – people who knew me and who knew Alex – would avert their eyes when they saw me around the village, and this compounded my already fragile, broken heart. It would have been kind for them to pass time with me, to speak of Alex instead of choosing to walk past. My son lived, he existed, he died, he mattered. Why do many struggle to mention the name of the deceased? I spent many hours following Alex's funeral curled up in a ball on the floor, alone, burying my head in Alex's favourite sweatshirt. Steve had returned to work, Tom resumed his studies in Newcastle to complete his university degree, and James went back to primary school. It was so kind of those few mums who were in touch, whose children had grown up alongside Alex or who had been coffee or dinner-party friends of mine when our kids were younger. However, I never again heard from most of the local mums who attended the funeral and knew Alex as a child. Perhaps this was as a result of their judgement for my divorce and re-marriage some ten years earlier. Or maybe their silence was a result of the awkwardness that surrounds the shock and horror of the sudden death of a child or young adult – approaching the bereaved can feel daunting. I was incapable of asking for anything, as I was almost too raw and devastated to speak, but just to receive their kindness would have meant so very much. Some pretended not to notice me in the village, yet I could see their discomfort. On more than one occasion, a mum I had known very well had turned the other way as I approached. I have sometimes wondered how this ostracizing behaviour sat with their children, young adults and peers of Alex's, and whether they would act differently than their parents, given similar circumstances. There were, however, a few exceptions, and I will be forever grateful for their friendship and compassion at that time. To those few who did not ignore me, thank you. You helped me face another hour, another day when I was not sure I could survive.

Around four months after Alex's death, an old school friend came into my mind. I had kept in touch with her, albeit infrequently over the years, and we occasionally met to catch up. Both of our eldest sons were born just eight weeks apart, and it occurred to me that she might not know of Alex's death, as I had not heard from her. I called her, something I hated doing, as the words never become less painful to say. In answering the phone to me, she did not say how sorry she was, so I assumed she did not know. I carefully started to tell her my shocking news when she said she had heard of Alex's death several months prior. I terminated the conversation as quickly as possible once I realized that she already knew but had made no attempt to contact me, despite us knowing each other for 40 years. I was angry at myself for trying to gently tell her my horrific news when she did not deserve my thoughtfulness. It is so true that you are often disappointed by people you thought you knew when the worst happens.

However, this provided me with some unexpected gifts: clarity to find my inner strength and resilience, and learning what my levels of endurance are when faced with the worst. Few people, fortunately for them, have the opportunity to discover their own limits.

A short while later, I bumped into one mum I knew whose son was a few years older than Alex, and I told her that Alex had recently died. She stared at me with a fixed smile on her face, ignoring my words and the pain in my eyes when she replied enthusiastically, "And my son got married recently." When you are heartbroken, insensitivity is hard to deal with, and I was wounded by her bungled and cruel reaction.

About six months after Alex's death, a "friend" saw me sitting alone, red-eyed in a cafe and asked me, in a slightly irritated fashion, "What's wrong?" I told her, somewhat apologetically, that I was thinking of Alex, who she had known as a young boy when he attended the same primary school as her sons. "Oh," she curtly replied, "I thought something else had happened." Each time I saw her after that, she tried to avoid me or seemed annoyed with my sadness and frankly bored by my grief. My son's death appeared to frustrate her, as I was not yet "over it" after six months. Grief is not like a broken leg. Just because it cannot be seen, it does not mean that the pain is not there. It doesn't heal like a shattered bone, either – it lasts a lifetime.

One former friend and neighbour looked mortified when he saw me approaching him on the pavement the day after Alex's funeral. He then said to me quite brightly, "Alright?" I stared at him trying to process his thoughtlessly breezy and inappropriate one-word question and opened my mouth to reply, but no words escaped. Probably for the best! Thereafter, his wife avoided me whenever our paths crossed, and they never spoke to me again. As several of this group are churchgoers – some regular, some less so – their lack of kindness struck me as surprising. There will be those who recognize themselves in these descriptions, should they ever read my book, and yet I make no apology for exposing these uncomfortable truths.

We, the survivors of suicide, have all likely had the visit from the nosey "friend" whose mission was to discover all they could about the deceased child. They often catch you at your most vulnerable, appearing out of nowhere and disappearing just as quickly. They are called grief tourists, and I, unfortunately, was not wise enough nor strong enough to turn one such tourist away at my door.

Surprisingly and sadly, I did not receive a condolence card, text, phone call, visit or hear anything from the family of Alex's best childhood friend who lived nearby. The boys were close in primary school and regularly spent time at each other's houses, and our families knew each other well. When the mother was ill several years before, I baked a cake, took flowers and went to offer my support despite our boys moving onto different friendship groups by that time. To hear nothing was heartless and felt like Alex's friendship had never mattered, that he never mattered and, worse, that his death did not matter despite those earlier years of close friendship.

Another layer of pain was added by two of the people closest to me, a relative and a friend, both of whom chose to fade away from my broken life within a few months of Alex's death. I had supported them through their difficulties many times, now so seemingly trivial compared to the enormity of my child's death. I was discarded when I was at my most vulnerable and the most broken that it is possible for a human being to be. My first birthday after losing Alex was especially horrific, knowing that there would be no card and no phone call from my precious son and knowing that, in just days, we would be flying to Canada to scatter his ashes on his birthday. To have been cared for on that awful day by those two people who lived nearby and who had not seen me for months would have been a deeply appreciated kindness, but they chose not to give it. This felt especially cruel.

Losing Alex was worse than losing them a million times, though, and it taught me that their decision to abandon me could not be allowed to bring me down further. I had to survive this for the sake of Tom, James and Steve. Their unkindness left me sad, but I can hear Alex's voice of reason and maturity, telling me to let it go. Tom has encouraged me to accept the things you cannot change and to bear no grudge for their inability to be compassionate and supportive. It is an uncomfortable truth that, when tragedy strikes, you cannot assume who will remain present in your life. Both Tom and I knew what Alex would have said – we could even hear him saying it: "Forget them, they are not worth it." As I now have limited mental space for additional pain, I have let it go, and, instead, I prefer to focus on the kindness that you do encounter. It is such a joy when you do.

"Do you have any other advice?" asked the boy.
"Don't measure how valuable you are by the way you are treated,"
said the horse.
Charlie Mackesy, The Boy, the Mole, the Fox and the Horse

However, despite these additional hurts, I have come to believe that often unkindness is not the intention in many encounters. Instead, this behaviour stems from ineptitude or lack of compassion in someone else's tragedy. Put simply, certain people cannot handle such deep pain and choose instead to run from it. It is generally accepted that we, as a race, do not deal well with death. Those of us who are living with the worst bereavement, that of losing a child, are testament to many similar, seemingly cruel experiences. As I have mentioned before, to reach out takes a special kind of person. It is surprising to me how many people, mostly those around my own middle age, including several in caring professions, were completely unable or unwilling to do this.

If you're wondering how to help a grieving parent, I would urge you not to do nothing – a double negative, I know. So, putting it another way: do something! Any act of kindness, however small, will be remembered and greatly appreciated. When someone's whole world has imploded, and when their heart is torn into a million pieces, be kind. Then, be kind some more. When you're grieving, there will be those who cross the street to avoid you, those who avert their eyes, those who drop you, and those who let you down even though you thought you could rely on them for support when the worst happens in your life. The essence of any relationship, however close or casual that relationship might be, is giving. The most welcome and beautiful thing you can do is to give – make a cake, take a few flowers, maybe a card or just share a cup of tea. You do not need to have fancy words, as there are none at the most devastating time imaginable.

"What do you want to be when you grow up?"
"Kind," said the boy.
Charlie Mackesy, The Boy, the Mole, the Fox and the Horse

The social freezing-out and intentional rejection from some is also a sadly common theme, but I prefer to focus on the good that is all around me. I have learnt that only I have the power to release myself from past hurts, and this is enlightening. In walking through this grief, you never really know how anyone will react when your child dies, nor can you predict who will remain by your side and who will not. It may be that some people are just not capable of sharing that painful journey with you, and this gives you clarity, a gift I wish I had not had to receive.

I have had to re-evaluate relationships, withdraw from those that cause additional pain and become more selective about who I let into my life. I simply have enough agony to live with – there is no room for more. To damage my resilience – already in shreds – is to crush me, and for James and Tom's sakes especially, I have sought to avoid this. This is where living by the sea has come to soothe my broken heart when no human was able to. I had to discover it myself, and strangely I knew what I needed from the earliest days of losing Alex: to be near the ocean. I am equally soothed by the peace and tranquillity of the gentle waves lapping on the beach on a tranquil day as I am beside the fierce, noisy and magnificent waves lashing the shoreline in stormy weather. Whatever the season, being beside the ocean is my favourite place to be, especially early in the morning when it is quiet, and I am alone with my chats with Alex and the memories I cherish.

I have come to see that I am largely on my own with my grief, and perhaps that is how it should be, as I alone had that special relationship with my beloved son. Once death broke that, I have had to navigate my new relationship with Alex. He will always be a large part of my life and will live within me until my final breath. Love remains forever, as does the pain, but I will never forget the love, the smiles and the unbreakable connection I have with Alex.

"I find the loss very hard to bear… Everything has lost its meaning to me… the acute sorrow after such a loss will run its course, but also we will remain inconsolable, and will never find a substitute… and that is how it should be. It is the only way of perpetuating a love that we do not want to abandon.'

Sigmund Freud, *Mourning and Melancholia*, written after the death of his daughter and four-year-old grandson

CHAPTER 9

LIVING WITHOUT ALEX

I thought long about the title for this chapter and, although I settled on "Living Without Alex," it does not quite fit with how I really feel. Although it is agonizingly real that Alex is no longer a physical presence in our lives, he remains a huge part of my day and is kept forever in my heart. Of course, I accept that Alex is dead, although each and every time I either say, think or write those shocking words, it never seems to become less painful. I know he is gone forever, and yet I almost feel that he is going to call me, and we can plan a visit together soon. I don't even need to close my eyes to recall everything that made him Alex. This is like a never-ending cycle of yearning amidst the harsh truth and hateful reality. Living without my son's physical presence is like living with an amputation of a limb, except losing your child is a million times worse. I wish I had lost a limb and not my wonderful son.

I think that I still feel a sense of denial, and perhaps this helps me survive by giving me respite from my grief. I try not to cocoon myself for more than a few brief moments, as to do so serves only to bring me to a crashing low when reality rears its head once more. I can totally relate to the words of Sir Bob Geldof talking about the loss of his daughter Peaches:

"Time doesn't heal – it accommodates."

I also understand the sentiment shared by the retired world champion boxer Barry McGuigan as he describes his heartache at the death of his beloved daughter Danika from leukaemia:

"The pain of every day is the same."

These sentiments are my reality, too, as time passes from when Alex was alive. I wish it were now true that the memories of my son would make me smile, but it is not. I hope that day will come, but I cannot say when or if. Every memory of the too-brief time that I was Alex's mum on earth hurts so much. Of course, I will always be his mother, but not as I wish with all my heart I could be. I talk to him every day, usually when I am walking beside the sea near my new home in North Wales. I grew up here, and as my parents still live in the family home, Alex regularly spent time here as a young child. Each day I now walk past the spot on the promenade where I remember him enjoying *Punch and Judy*.

The inescapable sorrow of Alex's life ending is with me every second, but perhaps, in time, the grief might lessen in its intensity. I owe it to Alex's memory and to his brothers to pick up the pieces of my destroyed life. No matter what, I will always have an emotional relationship with my first born. I loved him so deeply that my pain matches the depth of that love. Alex will always be my son despite him dying. He is with me always, and I will love him and be his proud mum forever.

The daily ache of Alex's absence in my life lingers and never goes. The death of a child is always tragic and losing a child in such a sudden and shocking way ages a parent. I am no exception to these visible changes, and I am unsurprised to learn that research says that parents who lose children face a higher risk of early death. The bereaved parent has to make a commitment to life, and the hardest part of that new life is facing every new day whilst also facing the reality that your adored child is still dead. Milestones are especially painful, as there will be no more for Alex, and he will forever be 23 years old. As Alex's peers go forward in life, get married and have children, there will be no such happy events for us. I find grocery shopping especially painful as Alex's birthday approaches. To see Alex's birthday as the sell-by date on products is a dagger to my heart, and I still cannot buy products labelled with it. I suspect that this will always be difficult for me.

There will always be one son missing in my life despite having three in my heart. My longing for Alex will never cease, just as my love for him will never lessen. My life has fallen into a natural rhythm of moving forward, not moving on. We all grieve differently, and grief is unique. The misconception by others who have not lost a beloved child is that time heals our pain, yet I do not accept that it does. Instead, it absorbs into who we are, changes us and lives within us forever.

In the early days and weeks following his brother's death, Tom tried valiantly to ease my pain, and I know he will not mind me saying that it was difficult for him to learn that he could not. My loving, wonderful middle son has had to accept that he cannot lessen the anguish I feel every day over losing his big brother. He also knows that a large space in my heart is permanently reserved for Alex – the space that was already his will always belong to him. Tom continues to try to ease me back into life with his gentle encouragement to seek acceptance and peace. He explained that not to do so was hurting him, and he and James deserve to still have their mum.

Living without Alex is like living in two parallel universes: the gut-wrenching one where I know that Alex is dead and not coming back, and the other, which I want to believe is true, where he is still living in Canada, skiing on the mountain he loved, living in his flat on that same peak, cycling and working. Even now, I can be caught off guard if I see someone who resembles Alex because I hope for all of this to have been a nightmare from which I will wake up. In fact, I stared in stunned silence when, two years after Alex's death, my husband prepared me for the sight of one of the young men who arrived to help us move from Cheshire to North Wales. I have never before or since seen anyone who looked more like Alex, and I was transported to my previous life, if only for the briefest of seconds. The crushing reality that Alex will never be alive again is excruciating and lands me back in the painful world I now inhabit. These stomach punches have eased as reality and acceptance take hold, only to be replaced by a constant nausea and feeling of isolation from the rest of the world. The horror of Alex's death still has the ability to drag me back to when my world fell apart.

In my darkest hours since Alex died, I know that I am battling against my own efforts to shut down, as the pain inside me is relentless and indescribable. I have never suffered from depression, and each day I can still appreciate beauty in nature. You might have thought that I would not succumb to dark thoughts, yet perhaps I am not as strong as I thought. Unless you, too, have experienced losing a child to suicide, you cannot judge. I try so hard for Tom and James to be the loving, supportive mum they deserve, and I believe that their lives are repairing and will be happy and fulfilling. Sometimes, I wonder if I am just a failure at handling grief, at being the mum of a deceased child. If only the pain could leave me for an hour, a day, but it is always with me, as is my love for Alex. Perhaps the two go hand in hand. "If only heaven had visiting hours," to quote Ed Sheeran, my allowance would be booked in already...

I was struck by the familiarity of the words spoken by the grieving mother of tragic plane crash victim, 28-year-old footballer Emiliano Sala, who, shortly before his untimely death, had signed for Cardiff City Football Club. He was also the eldest of three children, and she said, "The pain will never go away. I am practically dead while living." I totally understand her words. The intense pain that reaches deep inside you, that is there every second of the day and night, has not gone for me, but you learn to acclimatize yourself to the pain so that you appear to be coping to the outside world. The reality is not quite as it seems, though.

In the second year after Alex's death, we decided to take a family holiday. By now, Tom had completed his degree (for which he received first-class honours – Alex would have been so proud of his younger brother), and we needed a week away just to be together. I chose to visit the stunning Outer Hebrides, and we spent a wonderful week on the Isle of Harris and Lewis. As I have said before, the ocean seems to bring me a welcome connection to Alex, and the unspoilt beaches of these beautiful isles were a haven. I felt so connected to this isolated landscape, and I really feel that Alex led me there. Perhaps he knew what we needed, and it was here on these powder-white sandy beaches that we walked, watched the boys play football, ran in the wind, ate wonderful fresh food, and enjoyed such warm hospitality. I watched Tom take James kayaking and, with tears in my eyes, I saw the two surviving brothers strengthen their bond. This fed my soul and gave me the first sparks of hope that we could endure our tragedy. It warmed me to see the boys laughing together, jovially teasing each other, and yet, at other times, their eyes glistened with tears for their absent big brother, who they loved so much and alongside whom they would now never grow old. These islands and the special people we met will forever retain a place in my heart for giving me hope of a future without Alex. It still tears me apart to write those words and, of course, he will always be an integral part of our family – but it can never be the same.

My time on earth with Alex was only to be 23 years, 4 months and 10 days, nowhere near enough. I recollect the words from *Toy Story*, one of Alex's favourite childhood films: "To infinity and beyond." The love I have for Alex will remain inside me until infinity and beyond.

Alex was on loan to me, as all children are, and I am reminded of the words of Kahlil Gibran:

> *"Your children are not your children.*
> *They are sons and daughters of life's longing for itself.*
> *They come through you but not from you.*
> *And though they are with you, yet they belong not to you."*

Sometimes I succumb to the grief and focus on the "if only." If only he had waited for my trip to Canada, if only he had shared his suffering with me or a friend, if only he had not told me he was fine, if only I had jumped straight on a plane days before he died when I thought it would be fine to go the following week… if only I had listened more to my inner voice telling me something was not right, if only I had not thought I had a lifetime with my dear son to help if something was wrong. If only he had made a different choice. What did I miss? Every loving word we spoke during that last phone call, every nuance, every pause will remain with me until my last breath. I live with the anguish of asking myself how Alex could have made such an irrevocable decision without admitting to me that he did have a problem.

Alex must have felt isolated, lonely and even ashamed of the pain and dysfunction that blighted his final two years following his circumcision. Tragically, he felt unable to reach out to any of his good friends in Canada or to me – the person who loved him more than anyone in the world, and this I know he knew. I had frequently told Alex, as I do Tom, that my phone is beside me, and I am available always, anytime. I ask myself often, "Why didn't you tell me, Alex? You needed me, and I was there, if only you had let me in." Sadly, Alex only found it possible to describe his suffering when he was close to ending his life. I replay the sadness and trauma of his last hours and minutes as I have learnt more about them. I stood in his bedroom in Canada just three days after his death, knowing that this was where the life of the son I loved with all my heart had ended.

I try my best to bat these thoughts away as they serve no purpose and only to torture me. Alex would be cross with me, and he tried his best in his last email to tell me his death was not my fault. I can be consumed by different narratives. I did fly out to Canada that night of our last telephone call and arrived in time to save him. I became his saviour, the mum who makes everything all right, whose love for him is enough to keep him safe. But sadly, that is not what happened, and I will always feel guilt. As I have said before in this book – and it is worth repeating for other bereaved parents stuck on self-blame – I did my best with the information I had. Alex asked me in his last email to publicize his suffering in order to help others, and doing this helps to ease a little of my guilt for not saving him.

I heard it said by a parent whose daughter died that we have words for a wife whose husband has died, or a husband whose wife dies, or children who have lost both parents, but there is no word in the English language to describe those of us whose child has died. I believe that is because the horror and pain are beyond words. However, on researching this, I discovered that there is a word, albeit uncommonly known and not of the English language. It is from

Indian Sanskrit, the world's oldest language and the sacred language of Hinduism, from which it is believed all others have originated. It is *vilomah*, and it means "against the order", which, indeed, the death of a child is.

When I talk to Alex, I sometimes smile as his wit and humour were a prominent part of his character. I know what he would have said about many subjects and have many of his witty remarks to revisit. Whilst I admit that such memories are followed by tears at my loss, perhaps in time the memories will envelop me as he did in a warm hug. I have always felt Alex with me, wherever I am in the world.

During the early hours of the morning around four months after Alex died and in my half-awake state, I became aware of Alex's presence at the foot of my bed. He was half turning to face me and was smiling at me. Words were unnecessary, and he did not speak, but he was definitely saying to me, either through his eyes or his smile or some other mode of communication, "I am alright, Mum, I am at peace." I have hoped and waited for Alex to appear before me again, but sadly he has not.

I keep Alex's belongings in memory boxes in a wardrobe in the spare bedroom and have only looked at them a handful of times, as I find it too harrowing. I deliberately keep a favourite sweatshirt on the top of one box so that I can just lift the lid and bury my head in it, as it still smells a little of him – or more probably, the soap powder he used in Canada. This is my most cherished item, apart from two others: a bookmark he made for me one Christmas when he was in primary school and the lock of his hair that I gently cut from his still body after his death, my most treasured possession of all.

I have such a good memory, and this is both a blessing and a curse: a blessing because nothing is forgotten, yet a curse because I can recall everything from my pregnancy to the day he died. It adds to my profound sadness that these memories are exactly that, memories, in the past, never to be added to with new ones. So many times since Alex died, I have heard people say that the memories will be a comfort, and yet I find them excruciating, as it just affirms that my boy is gone forever. In time I hope these memories will bring happiness.

It was always heart-wrenching to part with Alex when he returned to Canada or when I returned from Canada. It felt as though I was leaving a part of myself behind. I was mercifully unaware that the strength I needed to cope with these farewells would be nothing compared to what was to come. Some of my most treasured memories are of our hugs. I knew that my lovely boy would hug me as soon as he saw me, and this was fully worth my apprehension at flying across an ocean alone. These hugs are now eternally unattainable, yet the feeling of love and joy that this brought me will remain with me always.

I recently read some poignant words by the British columnist Sarah Vine that resonated with me. She was lamenting the passage of time as her own children were approaching adulthood, and I was struck by how it is especially devastating for us bereaved parents, who will never again even see our beloved children:

What we want is what we don't have: time. The chance to slow the clocks, perhaps freeze the moment, until we're finally ready to let go. And maybe even given the opportunity to do it all again, only without the mistakes. The chance to re-sit that great defining test of adulthood, being a parent, and to pass with flying colours. Because the truth is, you never quite get it right. I don't think any parent reaches their child's 18th birthday without wishing they had done some things differently.

I have learnt that grief can manifest in physical symptoms. Lack of sleep has become my new normal, and I rarely manage more than four hours a night. On waking, my head refills with the sickening reality, and I often wake in the night hours with a racing heart, which takes several minutes to slow down. At first, I thought perhaps it was a cardiac issue – not that I cared – but have since read that after a massive, unexpected trauma, physical symptoms can be expected. It is not unusual for me now to find myself short of breath, momentarily unable to inhale sufficiently, and this can be alarming, as it feels like I cannot take in enough oxygen. I have learnt that anxiety and panic attacks, both of which I am now familiar with, are not uncommon symptoms when bereaved. Again, I have never suffered from depression, and I have not resorted to sleeping tablets, anti-depressants or any other form of medication to cope with my grief – unless chocolate counts? I do understand that for many, anti-depressants are the answer, just not for me. I am grieving, but I am not depressed. Our bodies react in different ways to grief, and I now understand that, in navigating my son's death, there are times when I experience physical responses to this nightmare, and these are now a part of my life.

As previously mentioned, group therapy was not for me. I understand that it can be a lifeline for many bereaved parents, but individual therapy was a better fit once I found the right counsellor. Individual therapy provided a safe place to cry, talk about Alex and begin to come to terms with the enormity of his death. I am so grateful for how my weekly visits were the start of putting myself back together.

I used to love life and its joy, but since Alex died, I have found myself just existing, even if I can still appreciate the views from my home of the Welsh mountains and of the nearby sea. Daily coastal walking has had a positive effect on my mental health and soothes me every day. This routine has been the best prescription I could have given myself as I slowly piece my broken heart and life back together. Sometimes I merely succeed in creating a mask of normality and, when the mask slips, I sink lower that I ever thought it possible.

Victor E. Frankl, the renowned psychiatrist, wrote a book called *Man's Search for Meaning*, which has helped me to process Alex's suffering and understand how it consumed his entire existence. He describes suffering as omnipresent and uses an analogy of the behaviour of gas to explain suffering:

If a certain quantity of gas is pumped into an empty chamber, it will fill the chamber completely and evenly, no matter how big the chamber. Thus, suffering completely fills the human soul and conscious mind, no matter whether the suffering is great or little. Therefore, the size of human suffering is absolutely relative.

I have had to accept that I cannot turn back time, however much I long to do just that. I cannot bring Alex back. I am learning to accept this and to forgive Alex for not only leaving me, but also for not giving me the chance to help him. I recognize that Alex's tragic, irrevocable act of killing himself will forever impact my life, and I will forever mourn him. I have struggled with acceptance and still have moments when I feel almost, but not quite, that Alex has not gone forever. Certainly, I feel him close to me, but that is different from feeling that he will come back. This is the worst part of death. The finality and brutality of this is excruciating, and I make no apology for mentioning again that kindness is the most beautiful gift you can offer bereaved parents, who have no choice but to live the rest of their lives with the pain of horrific loss.

*"Be kind whenever possible.
It is always possible."*

Dalai Lama

*"Kindness is the greatest wealth of all. Small acts
of kindness last longer than a lifetime."*

Eddie Jaku

CHAPTER 10

WHAT TO SAY (AND NOT TO SAY) TO A GRIEVING PARENT

People far away can move closer, and those close can move away and even disappear from your life. But no matter who you are, please know you can help someone who is grieving. Child loss is like no other. A bereaved parent's good days are so much more painful than you could ever imagine. Here are my words of advice. I wish with all my heart that I did not feel qualified to offer them:

Do not worry about saying the wrong thing, as you will sometimes get it wrong and saying something is braver and less wounding than saying nothing. Do not avoid the bereaved person, who feels lost and isolated enough as it is. The feeling that someone cares about you and your loss is so comforting, and just hearing the words "I am so sorry" is more welcome than you could know. Often, this is the only gift a suicide parent needs. Let the bereaved talk about their child. Remember, you only have to listen to this for a very short time, maybe for just a handful of minutes. This is the bereaved parent's new life, forever. And if you are a parent, they are living your worst nightmare. Alternatively, a simple note, a simple gesture can make a huge difference. Even now, more than three years after Alex's death, there are still some days when the only comfort I can find is re-reading the sympathy cards I received and for which I am so grateful.

It takes a lifetime to grieve the death of a child, and I will be grieving Alex for the rest of mine. Compassion and love, not advice, are needed. Please do not push a bereaved parent to move on because you care about them or because it would make you feel more comfortable. Either way, unless you have walked this painful path, you are not qualified to suggest to someone that "it is time to move on." It is offensive when you do. I never will, and especially not just to make you feel better. Instead, I have learnt that life grows around the pain. Every bereaved parent is different, as are the relationships they had with their deceased child.

Additionally, the circumstances of losing a child will be different, and each situation can alter the path to grief and acceptance. Please don't pressure a bereaved parent to begin to heal until they are capable. They will become more able to act out the role expected by others, and I can certainly attest to this. The reality inside can be very different. Unfortunately, I am writing these words from the experience of being told by a visitor to my home that it was time that I was moving on from the acute grief stage, and this was within mere months of Alex's death.

Say the name of the dead child and speak of him. Promise that he will never be forgotten. This is the best comfort, to talk about him, his likes and dislikes. Share memories if you have them. Do not worry about upsetting the bereaved by mentioning their dead child's name. You cannot upset someone any more than they already are, and by avoiding his name due to your discomfort, you are causing further pain. To mention a deceased child's name is to respect and honour their life, and this helps the grieving mother or father. Just as parents of living children love them unconditionally forever, so do the bereaved. Two years after Alex's death, a few mums were discussing their experiences of childbirth, but when I joined in and mentioned Alex's birth, there was an uncomfortable silence, and the conversation was swiftly moved on by others. I felt hurt, isolated, incredibly lonely and sad. Allow Alex to be present sometimes; it is all I have. I want to speak about my deceased child as normally and often as you speak of your living ones. Sadly, it seems this is embarrassing, almost taboo in our society, and I hope this can change.

On the subject of emojis in text messages to a heartbroken parent, they are inadequate, too easy, inappropriate and just plain wrong.

Allow a grieving parent to be unpredictable. Having said that I would ask you to listen while I share memories of my beloved boy, please accept when I need to stop. If I change the subject, it is because the pain of the memories has become too enormous in that moment.

Try to be sensitive about using the word "heartbreak". Often it refers to something that is not. If I had a pound for every person who has told me of their heartbreak at an older relative's death... With respect, your bereavement may be extremely sad to you, but an elderly person's death and a life well-lived is not heart-breaking, unlike the death of a child or young adult. I understand, however, that unless you have survived the death of your son or daughter, you may not accept these sentiments.

Please do not infer that suicide is selfish. My son was the least self-centred human you could meet. Loving, gentle, caring – I could continue with a list of his qualities, at the forefront of which was empathy to the suffering of others. However, he was suffering hugely both physically and emotionally, and tragically, his despair overwhelmed his desire for life.

Don't say, "Time heals." It doesn't, in my opinion. Grief is eternal when you lose a child. The searing intensity barely abates, but you do become better at keeping your pain to yourself, then allowing it to be released when you are alone.

Don't ever impose your timeline on someone else's grief. Some people need more time than others, and no one person's time frame is correct. If you are in a family that is grieving, don't feel guilty if you are mending while someone else is still deep in their anguish. Time has made me accept grief will always be by my side. After more than three years of being a bereaved parent, I now know that my sadness is only about me, and nobody else knows what is best for me. Grief is as unique as the wonderful child you have lost.

Don't just show up at the bereaved parent's house a few weeks after the tragedy, asking questions and learning the details. In my shocked, exhausted and heartbroken state, I bared my soul and shared my pain with people who I never heard from again.

Accept that holidays, birthdays, Mother's Day, Christmas and especially the deceased child's birthday will forever be painful for the grieving parent. I have found my birthday to be especially difficult, as Alex sent such lovely cards with his familiar handwriting and loving words. My child will be forever absent and will never share those special dates again. This is excruciating. It is so thoughtful to send a little message or note. Thank you to those who have done this – I am grateful. You will never know how much it has helped me get through such difficult and significant dates.

Follow through on the promises you make to the bereaved. Do not be like a mum of one of James' school friends who, in the days following our loss, said she would be in touch to invite him for tea but never was. Also don't be like that same mum who sent a lovely, long text upon hearing of my son's death saying how much you will "be there to lift me up when I fall." I thanked her and never heard from her again. My sad, grieving little ten-year-old would have loved to be invited out for tea, especially in those early weeks when he came home from school to find me inconsolable with grief. Thank you to those few who did invite James for tea or to your home to play. It gave me some relief to know that my lovely little boy was enjoying a normal few hours with his friends when home was such a sad place to be. It was a strain to be the mum he needed at that time, yet I tried to ensure that he knew he was loved, although that seemed somehow inadequate. I was not able to appear happy. That was impossible, and this must have been difficult for him and is often still our reality. Parents of a child who has died with a younger sibling at home need play date invitations. They give the parent space to grieve, and this is one of the kindest things you can do for them. I will not forget those who provided this.

Survivors crave an ocean of love just to face each day with the turmoil in their heart, and it takes special, compassionate people to provide this. Grief needs kindness, and little gestures create huge ripples. It still seems sad to me that those who I never heard from again after they attended Alex's funeral would be the first to support a church function or rightly have compassion for suffering around the world. Yet I was a fellow human, a local mum, shattered into a million pieces, totally heartbroken and right on their doorstep. When you are deranged with grief, avoidance is excruciating and exacerbates the isolation and darkness.

That last point reminds me of my next…

Don't put your mobile phone number on the church attendance card at the funeral with a note to call you if I need anything. While it may seem a helpful sentiment, the bereaved probably will not let you know, so think of something nice and just do it. I was not in a fit state to ask and didn't know what I needed, apart from my son not to be dead.

Please do send a condolence card as these bring an enormous amount of comfort. Thank you, thank you, thank you to everyone who sent one to me − I treasure them all.

Be careful of what you write inside of these cards, though. Only one person in scores and scores of lovely messages of condolence said how sorry they were to hear of Alex's suicide. Whilst this was indeed how Alex died, I wonder why you wrote that and not as everyone else did, to simply express sadness at Alex's death? It felt like a cruel emphasis and not relevant. Would you have also referenced someone's fatal heart attack or car crash in your sympathy card? Please do not define Alex's life by his death. He was so much more than that.

I have also learnt that, sadly, it is not uncommon for key relationships to change following a tragic death of a child. The horrific trauma and shock amplified cracks in relationships, and those that were not solid completely disappeared. In my two closest female friendships, texts and offers to meet for coffee started to cool off very soon after Alex's death and, within a few months, they ceased altogether. Until you have to face the unthinkable, you can never truly know who will be there to catch you when you fall. It is perhaps only then that you accept what you had suspected before but failed to truly see. I had no choice that my son died, but you did have a choice to be a good support, and you chose not to be.

One of the most moving acts of humanity happened only a few weeks after Alex's death, when the lovely local butcher saw me while I was sitting in my car with the window open. He said nothing, reached for my hand and held it, looking into my eyes with such kindness and compassion. No words were necessary and we both, as parents, understood this. It can be the seemingly insignificant moments of connection that mean the most. Thank you, I will never forget that moment of human connection at its best.

Don't try to understand because you can't. Just be kind.

Leave little care packages: a cake, a few flowers, a thoughtful card, anything that would make them feel cared for and less desperate and alone. Be your kindest self, as the bereaved will always remember and be forever grateful.

Do not judge a person's grief. Everyone deals with it differently. Just because someone is not behaving the way you think you would, it does not mean it is wrong. Just because they have one good day, don't expect the next to be the same. Grief comes in waves, good and bad. Hopefully, you will never know how you would act if your child died.

Please don't minimize a person's pain, sugar-coat it or try to put a positive spin on the conversation. For me, there isn't one, and nothing you can say will make it any better. I do not want to hear that my darling boy is "in a better place." I just want him not to be dead. There is no need for you to explain my grief with quotes or clichés; it doesn't help, and it trivializes my loss.

Don't tell a grieving parent that they are strong. In my case, I feel as broken as a smashed vase every day.

Do not be a wicked troll. I have been horrified by some sick messages attached to the online story of Alex's suffering. You are inhuman and deserve no space here.

To lose a child by suicide, or in any shocking way, is more traumatic than anything. Close your eyes and imagine the policeman knocking at your door and telling you that your adored child is dead. Imagine the agony and how your whole world implodes in those seconds. Then multiply that by a zillion, and you still won't even come close to the true pain. I feel that loss and that deep despair every day, every night, every minute, and that has not changed.

To outlive your child reveals those around you who will be there to support you. This is perhaps best summed up by Eddie Jaku in his inspiring memoir, *The Happiest Man on Earth*:

There are always miracles in the world, even when all seems hopeless. And when there are no miracles, you can make them happen. With a simple act of kindness, you can save another person from despair, and that might just save their life. And this is the greatest miracle of all.

"Hope tells us that life is full of darkness and suffering — and yet if we survive today, tomorrow we'll be free."

Edith Eger, *The Gift*

CHAPTER 11

MEANING AND HOPE

What do you do when you lose one of the people you love with all
your heart, who gave your life meaning? My new world of grief
had no purpose, and, for a time, I lost all hope. The passage of time
since Alex's death has led me to try to rediscover these things despite
my unimaginable pain.

I have come to recognize that I am lucky to have loved and
cherished my son so deeply and to have been loved by him in return.
I am grateful to have had the experience of being Alex's mum, albeit
for too short a time, and for the special moments when just a glance
between us was enough, when no words were necessary. We often
sniggered at a shared amusement or joke or more often, a sarcastic
witticism offered by Alex, who had an ability to see the humorous
side in many situations. Alex and I got each other, and this illuminates
lovely, shared moments, but also the tragedy of my knowing
something was wrong despite his protestations to the contrary. My
instinct did not quite fail me, rather it was me who failed to act upon
my instinct when it mattered most. To my eternal regret, my instinct
was telling me that all was not okay with Alex, yet I allowed him to
throw me off the scent with his false assurances. I will never forgive
myself for this.

Although this is the penultimate chapter of my book, there will
never be a final chapter of my love for Alex. His untimely death stole
away not only my beloved son, but also my dreams for his future
and the memories that would come with it. I have felt such sadness,
trauma and despair since losing my son that I have wished for death

to release me from the pain many times. I always knew, however, that this would be the last thing Alex would want; in fact, he would be furious with me, and a happy reunion in heaven or wherever would not await me! I have chosen life in the hope of rediscovering some happiness and for my love of my sons. I have found meaning in honouring Alex's last request of me by sharing his story with those contemplating circumcision and those suffering the adverse effects of the procedure. I do not want Alex's tragic death to have been in vain. My life will also have purpose if, through my words, I can help another bereaved family navigate the alien, cruel path of losing a beloved child to suicide.

My darling son lost all hope and that is what ended his life. However, his life and death had meaning. The devastating loss becomes incorporated into our new being. I am trying to do as those who have endured the agony of losing a child before me: to consciously remember and celebrate the 23 years, 4 months and 10 days I was lucky enough to have my darling son, and my love for him lives on. In accepting my grief and loss, I am gradually healing. I'm never going to return to who I was before, but I'm very slowly feeling grateful to have been Alex's mum.

I have found the strength to distance myself from shallow or one-sided relationships, and this has been an important part of my journey with grief. You have to rid yourself of people who cause you further heartache when you already have an overload of pain. I have also accepted that not everybody you wish to be kind, compassionate and supportive is capable, and losing a child does not inherently change those around you. When you come to realize this as a bereaved parent, it is a sign that you are in charge of your own needs when you had no control of keeping your beloved child alive. You can get through this agony if you find courage to know how to survive. Small steps…

For a long time, I was angry with the surgeon who performed Alex's circumcision. I repeatedly asked myself, *Was he negligent?* But anger is destructive and eats away at you, so I have had to let go of it and, in any case, nothing could bring Alex back to me.

Sadly, I know that there will be other bereaved parents of a beloved child who dies by suicide tomorrow, the next day and the day after that, just as there were many precious children and young adults who took their own lives before my son. It is my hope that my book will play a part, however small, in helping to remove the stigma of suicide. I encourage both compassion and understanding for the heartbroken parents left behind, and I have come to hope that, while the pain will never leave me, I may eventually accommodate it. Time has made me accept grief will always be by my side. The pain does become more manageable, and this provides hope that one day the agony will be less searing, and happy memories of your lost child will return. This is something I never would have thought possible three years ago, and I offer this hope to other bereaved parents. However, I feel a fraud as I type these words with tears streaming down my face, but I grasp onto the words of others who have trodden this heart-breaking path before me. US President Joe Biden suffered the tragic death of his wife and young daughter in a 1971 car crash and, 40 years later, he lost one of his sons who survived that accident to brain cancer. After his son's death, he said:

"The way you make it is you find purpose and you realize they're inside you. They're part of you. It's impossible to separate."

I try so hard to believe in these words and encourage other bereaved parents to retain hope in the knowledge that, in time, they will come to see that the love and memories of their child can never be taken away. I carry the essence of Alex with me every second of every day. To me, he is mine and forever a part of me. Love and grief are inextricably linked.

Healing requires us to let go of the guilt that we survivors of suicide feel. I have had to accept my own failings in not knowing of Alex's suffering. To other parents facing this agony, it may take the rest of your lives, but we have to see that we did our best with the information we had, and there was nothing we could have done to prevent our children's deaths. As I type those words, I feel slightly dishonest encouraging others to believe this, as my journey to accept this fact is far from complete. In fact, I may not ever believe that statement fully, but it is something I work on. I have not yet made peace with Alex's death, as that feels like accepting it was an inevitable outcome or even the right one for him, and I cannot feel that way. Perhaps one day I will, but I have made a conscious decision to live, to emerge from the darkness and you can, too, one minute at a time. I am learning that there is peace to be found in showing love and compassion to myself. I showered Alex with love all of his short life and did the best that I could. I am learning to forgive myself for not keeping my son alive. I am helped on this new discovery by those who care about how I am doing when I am not doing well. To other parents in this agonizing position, above all else, be the kindest person you can be to yourself.

I am trying hard to lock my wonderful memories of Alex in a secret room in my head where I hold the key and allow myself to enter when I need to. Thus far, I have failed to do this, as I have been largely living full-time in that space and can't bring myself to exit it. My rational mind is encouraging me to find a life outside of there, but my heart pulls me back constantly.

Perhaps the most difficult part of my grief has been accepting that Alex is not coming back. Tom especially has tried to lead me to a place of acceptance and encouraged me to see that there is peace to be found in doing so. Tom's continuing love, hope and faith in me have been the greatest of gifts and, these traits – together with his endless patience – have given me strength. I am convinced that both of my wonderful older sons are together guiding me toward healing, and a wise friend recently inscribed a book he gave me with the following heart-wrenching, wise words:

> *"Look after what you can look after, not after that which you cannot; and may you have the ability eventually to distinguish one from the other."*

I have found comfort in the words of Auschwitz survivor Edith Eger, who, when describing the hell of being a prisoner there, wrote:

"The very worst circumstances gave me the opportunity to discover the inner resources that helped me again and again to survive."

Losing a child is nothing like the experience of being a prisoner of war; it is a very different kind of nightmare, yet finding inner strength is vital for survival in both situations. I have found the strength because I have had to. It is not lost on me that the American Psychiatric Association ranks the trauma of losing someone you love to suicide as "catastrophic". I can sadly say that losing a child to suicide transports a parent into a living hell.

It is widely understood that there are five stages of grief, as defined by the acclaimed American-Swiss psychiatrist Elizabeth Kubler Ross. Whilst I relate to the different stages, the progress of my grief is far from linear, and I have visited each stage many times, backwards and forwards, and no doubt always will. My grief, as a so-called suicide survivor, is widely referred to as complicated grief and is quite different to the loss of an elderly relative. It is the death of our loved one plus the trauma of suicide that is so unbearable. It is taking me a longer time to engage with life again as I feel like I am on the outside of it all, but that is the nature of complicated grief. I seek isolation and my own company whenever possible, and my longing and sadness over Alex's death remains as intense as the night he died. Traumatic thoughts and images of the night he died are never far away, especially during the evening hours. I recognize in myself some of the symptoms of complicated grief, and I will seek further forms of therapy, as medication is not for me.

I have also found some comfort in the words of Mo Gawdat, whose beloved 21-year-old son Ali died in 2014. He said, "The gravity of the battle means nothing to those at peace." I believe that Alex has now found his peace and that his earthly suffering has ended, although I also feel that he is still on a journey, albeit in another place. I do believe that the soul lives forever, as does love, and that we are connected to something much greater than ourselves, although it's impossible to understand. I need to believe that one day I will be reunited with Alex, and I would describe this as my comfort blanket when I most need it, to reassure myself that, in the blink of an eye, we will be together again. I can hear Alex saying to me, "I was not yours to keep, Mum, I was mine. We will be together again when your time comes. Live your life, be the best parent to my brothers you can be, and don't blame yourself. Live a meaningful life." Some of those words were, indeed, the last Alex left for me on the evening of his death.

Music, especially my favourite pieces, does not yet bring me comfort, as I find it amplifies my pain. Despite this, there are songs that release my emotion and bring me moments of closeness to Alex. Now, I am thinking of "Smile" by Nat King Cole. The lyrics especially resonate as I do try to smile despite my breaking heart, forever remembering Alex's gorgeous smile in the sure knowledge that he is smiling upon me, a constant presence beside me.

Alex's death has given me a true understanding of the fleeting fragility of life, together with a respect that time is truly our most precious treasure. Gaynor Madgwick, in her very moving book *Aberfan: A Story of Survival, Love and Community in One of Britain's Worst Disasters*, quoted a story told to the mining tragedy's child survivors by the Reverend Irving Penberthy in his Sunday school. These words always bring a tear to my eye, yet also brought me comfort when my pain was too much to bear. I share them in the hope that it might bring comfort to others:

> *Billy Blackbird and Tommy Thrush were the best of friends. They always sang together in the morning, and they sang at many other times when they were happy. Tommy would often get carried away by his singing and would close his eyes and lift his head to the skies – but this was very dangerous. When he was young, Tommy's mother had often taught him to look left, look right, then left again, before singing to make sure that the coast was clear, but he often forgot.*
>
> *One day they went down to the village to find some crumbs: Tommy went into one garden and Billy went into the next. The weather was warm, and the garden was so full of flowers that Tommy was overcome with pleasure and, throwing back his head, he began to sing.*
>
> *But there was a crafty cat around, and cats can do very nasty things. This cat pounced upon Tommy and grabbed him by his claw. Billy heard*

his cries and came to his rescue. He pecked at the cat's head and ears, shrieking, "Let go!" until, at last, the cat let Tommy go and skulked away, leaving him badly hurt upon the ground.

Billy chirped his distress call and the other birds gathered, but there was little that they could do. They sent for the Red Cross Ravens, who took Tommy on a stretcher to Doctor Owl, who did his best to tend his wounds and treat him for shock.

When Billy went to visit him, Doctor Owl shook his head sadly and said, "There is no more I can do. He must go to the Land of Sunshine where the doves will be able to heal him."

"Where is the Land of Sunshine?" Billy asked.

"It is far beyond the distant mountains. I must send for the Eagle Express."

The Eagle Express soon arrived with a basket on his back and, when Tommy had been carefully placed in the basket, Billy waved goodbye, and the eagle soared into the sky.

When he had gone Billy turned to Doctor Owl and said, "Please tell me about the Land of Sunshine."

"It is a very wonderful place," said Doctor Owl. "The River of Life flows through the land with trees on its banks, and the leaves are for the healing of the nations."

"Have you been there, Doctor Owl?"

"Not yet, but I will go there one day and so will you," said Doctor Owl.

"It must be a very beautiful place," Billy sighed.

"It is. Some call it the 'Never-Never Land'. The sun never sets, the birds never fight, and they never grow old."

"No cats?" said Billy.

"I really don't know the answer to that," said Doctor Owl. "If there are cats, they will be cats with no claws who only eat cakes."

Billy looked into the distance and said, "When will Tommy come back?"

Doctor Owl smiled gently. "That's another thing about Never-Never Land," he said, "they never come back. That is where they belong." He held his wing out towards Billy comfortingly.

"You can't stay here in the forest forever, you know."

Billy asked, "What shall I do without my dear friend Tommy?"

"Just carry on singing," said Doctor Owl. "Tommy will be singing as well by the River of Life, but you must wait your turn."

So, Billy carried on singing in the forest and, somehow, Tommy did not seem so far away.

Once or twice, Billy thought he heard Tommy's song on the evening air, and he sang more loudly hoping that his friend might hear him too…

… and Billy did not feel so sad anymore.

I again find comfort in the words of President Biden:

"The time will come when a memory will bring a smile to your lips before it brings a tear to your eyes."

For me, this is something I long for, and these words give me hope that one day I, too, will reach this point. I can see some faint rays of light in my existence, most often during my daily walks along the seafront. There is something deeply spiritual and captivating about the ocean. It is where I now feel closest to Alex. I love the pounding of the crashing waves and frothy, white foam on a wintry day as much as the serenity and beauty of the still, blue sea when the sunshine appears to dance upon it. I meet other local walkers with whom I share this beautiful space as we enjoy the changing seasons on the ocean and often spot a seal or two as they play in the water by the shore. I grew up by the sea and have found solace in returning to it.

I don't take my life for granted; it is a gift to be cherished despite my inner pain. With Steve, Tom and James by my side, I am trying to walk back into life, and I feel Alex beside me with each step. While I know I will never truly recover from losing Alex, there have been brief moments when I have felt lucky because he was my son, albeit for too brief a time on this earth. He was my beautiful, placid, smiling baby; the loving, inquisitive toddler; the clever, sensitive boy; and the sometimes-grumpy teenager who became a wise, popular, hard-working, witty, caring, handsome, wonderful young man. They all left me, and I loved each one. I am gradually healing, never to return to who I was before, but very slowly feeling grateful for being Alex's mum.

Before I sat down this morning to finish the final paragraph of this book, I took a photograph of James on the last day of school before the summer holidays. His resemblance to Alex was not lost on me, but James is James, just as he should be. It is a comforting coincidence that this photograph appeared on my iPad directly below the last photograph of Alex and James together, almost as if Alex was watching over him. Watching James grow gives me reason to carry on and, along with Tom, he ensures that my life still has meaning.

An important aspect of publicizing Alex's story is to help other men suffering as he did and to inform others considering circumcision that the operation is not without risk. The UK charity 15 Square helps many men coping with the after-effects of circumcision, and I have contributed to their work in Alex's memory. It is important to ensure that men are aware that help and advice is available, and they are not alone. The most important part of my story as Alex's bereaved mum is not only to share my pain with other parents bereaved by suicide, but to emphasize the agony caused by suicide in the hope that it might just make one person not take this irrevocable step. I also want to offer hope. There is hope that those of us left behind can find meaning and purpose for our own lives whilst living alongside the pain. In those early days, weeks, months and yes, years, I would have said that was not possible. I have now seen that it is, but it is a choice you have to make and only you alone can make it – and it will be the hardest thing you will ever do.

I will never know if it was my beloved son's destiny to leave this earthly existence at such an early age. The shattering loss has broken my heart and changed my life irrevocably, but I have found the strength to write this book, which may offer other parents bereaved by suicide the hope that they too can survive this worst of tragedies. It is also my wish that my story will guide others to act decisively when I didn't and thereby help to save even one person from taking their own life. I also know that I have to do as Alex asked of me and share his story in the hope of helping other young men contemplating circumcision or who are suffering the adverse effects of circumcision. I will continue to tell my darling Alex's story so that his life and death have meaning.

Tom and James, Luskentyre 2018. Two brothers – there will always be three.

*"With feelings, there is no choice at all…
Grief is love's echo."*

Robert Webb, *How Not to Be a Boy*

CHAPTER 12

MY LETTER TO ALEX

My Darling Lix,

When I started writing in Canada, days after your death, I had no idea that those words would turn into a book. This has been the chapter that I have found the most agonizing, the most intimate and precious to write. You feel so close to me as I write with TC purring beside me. It is as though, despite your death, you and I are having one of our lovely chats. If I close my eyes, I can see your gorgeous, big green eyes approving my words, grinning, agreeing, groaning, offering advice and witty quips, sharing, laughing and cringing – often! I promised you, my darling, when I saw you in your coffin and slipped my hand into yours, that I would publicize your story to help others, just as you asked of me.

My journey as a mum began with you. You enriched my life in so many ways, and I will be forever thankful that I was your mum for the short time you were on this earth. I am grateful for the joy your birth brought me, and I will always cherish the memory of the loving, quiet, intelligent little boy you were, and the thoughtful, witty, interesting young man you became. I'll never forget the jokes that only you and I shared and the knowing look we gave each other when no words were needed. You had an adept sense of empathy for others, a quality we had in common. Do you remember buying me the film *The Notebook* for Mother's Day when you were 16 or 17? You had recently watched it on TV and were thoughtful enough to realize that it was something I would enjoy. How right you were. Of course the beautiful title track "Please Remember" by LeeAnn Rimes is heartbreakingly poignant. As if I will ever forget you, my darling. You were much loved by everyone, but most especially by me: I can see you grinning at that, but I know you would not dispute it! A mother's treasure is her child, and you were undoubtedly mine.

I know that you tried so hard to spare me your pain, choosing instead to endure it alone in the misguided belief that it would be easier for me to bear when you were gone. I can forgive you, as you were never a parent, and you could not have known how badly you misjudged that. I will miss you forever, and a part of me died with you. I know from your letter to me, and just from knowing and loving you, that you believed I would find the strength, if only for your brothers, to survive this agony. In this I have no choice, as I cannot let Tom and James down; they have lost so much in losing you, the big brother they loved so much, but they have also lost a part of me. The void you have left in our lives will never go, nor will the profound sense of loss and pain in a world without you.

I constantly reflect on our last phone call six days before you died and wonder how you appeared so normal when you perhaps knew it was to be our final conversation. I now think that you found peace in making the plan to end your suffering. I imagine you acknowledged that I was not totally convinced by your false reassurances that all was fine because we were so in tune. You understood the impact your death would have on me, and I thank you for your last loving words as you attempted to ease my inevitable pain. I know you want me to swap my tears for smiles when I think of you. Perhaps one day…

I am so, so sorry not to have been able to save you. While I have had to accept that you wanted to end your life and your suffering, I feel such guilt for missing something I should have seen as your mum. As the old saying goes, "Hindsight is a wonderful thing." I did have a sense of unease, but I just couldn't quite work out what it was. I had no idea of the depth of your despair and hoped that my imminent visit would help solve your worries. How wrong I was. I feel psychologically tortured as I ask myself repeatedly, *What could I have done differently? What signs did I miss? Should I have said more? Should I have said less? How could I have not known of your pain? How could you have done this to me?* The answer I tell myself constantly to the latter question is that you did not do this "to me." You chose not to live a life of continual suffering. You chose to end your pain. Both Ste and Tom have tried to make me accept that I did the best I could with the information I had.

If I could go back in time, knowing what I have since learnt about suicide and mental health, perhaps I could have saved you. I know that you found it so hard to ask for help despite being so very articulate. If only I had fully understood what you were really saying. I will never forgive myself for pushing the horror of my deepest fears to the farthest corner of my mind. It was as though obliterating the true horror of my uneasy feelings would make them untrue, except they were very real.

I worry that you cannot find total peace until I let you go, but this is my greatest struggle, as it is too unbearable. I am no longer afraid to die, as I hope and believe that we will be reunited one day. I know that you want me to focus on the happy memories, yet I am overwhelmed by the agony of losing you. Tom said we have to live your life through ours now, to find strength and joy as you wanted us to. Whilst I acknowledge Tom's words, how can I, knowing how much you suffered and hid it from everyone? I am so keen for your brothers to rediscover their happiness, and I know that they are on their way, but it feels different for me. I know that you would want me to suppress my deepest pain in front of your brothers, and this is challenging and not always possible. I know that you are encouraging me, and I can hear your voice guiding me to choose to live a meaningful life just as you wrote in your last words to me. I owe this to the three of you.

I am grateful to you for the letters you wrote explaining everything. You were so brave and selfless, my darling boy, and you fought so hard to spare us your pain. How I wish you had shared your agony. You said in your last email that you had to "free your soul from this torture" whilst emphasizing your love for me and "that it was not my fault." Even as you were contemplating your last hours alive, you were making sure that we knew you loved us. You never complained and were so full of courage. If anyone reading this feels that that is ironic, given how you ended your own life, then they did not know you. I can only imagine what strength it took for you to end your life. I know that you were worn down by your painful, relentless struggle to live. I know that you chose death as a release from your constant torment that had made life for you unbearable. I know that your soul was crushed, and the light within you dimmed following your circumcision. You became numb and disconnected. I saw it in your beautiful eyes on our last trip together and this, as you know, is why I repeatedly asked you how you truly were. You tried to convince me that you were fine, but I never really believed you, although I truly wanted to.

I admire you so much for taking full responsibility for hiding your pain, agreeing to the circumcision hastily without proper consideration, and ultimately choosing to end your life. I read your eloquent words and cried at your reason for agreeing to the surgery with the urologist you so disliked and who you did not adequately research. I wonder if you would not have proceeded had you done so. You were not to blame for accepting the medical advice to have a circumcision or for your subsequent suffering. Just as I chastise myself for not listening fully to my inner voice that something was wrong with you, I now know that you, too, wished you had listened to your inner voice that was telling you to run from this doctor. I can tell you, my darling son, that I insisted on an independent enquiry into your case in Canada – not an easy feat being so far away – and it took nine months. The outcome was that there was no proven negligence. We will never know, Lix, whether you were one of the unlucky ones for whom circumcision made a painful problem worse for no apparent reason, yet the number of men who have been terribly damaged by this surgery is alarming.

I often fantasize about a kinder world and think, if there was more kindness in ours, you might still be here. I ask myself, "Were you too good for this world?" From a very young age, you were special, compassionate and kind. So many who have died by suicide are described similarly, and I think there is something in that. You cared about disadvantaged people, the underdog, homelessness and sick children, and you hated cruelty to animals. I wish you could have heard all the love that was expressed for you in Canada when I met all of your friends and colleagues. One thing is certain Alex, we, your family and friends, truly are all the richer for having known and loved you.

Since your death, I have been horrified at some of the stories told to me by men of all backgrounds and ages following their circumcisions, and this has given me further motivation to publicize your experience, just as you asked of me. I know you would be pleased that the online article about you was the most read BBC News piece for a week. I am your voice now, and I vow to highlight the damage that may be caused by circumcision. In time, perhaps, this endeavour will help to ease some of my pain whilst contributing to your legacy.

I felt that you were in the room with me when I delivered my first speech as guest speaker at the AGM of the charity 15 Square. I think you would be proud of me for overcoming my nerves in order to share your story. If I can survive the trauma of the policeman at my door on the worst night of my life, then I can easily endure the discomfort of public speaking. After delivering my final sentence, applause erupted around the room. Some began to stand up, many in tears, and, eventually, the whole room was on their feet. I returned to my seat on the front row, head bowed, crying, feeling you beside me proudly watching.

I was recently asked to speak at the Worldwide Day of Genital Autonomy 2021 and was touched by the interest in, and respect for, your letter, as expressed by academics and medical experts from all over the world after I shared your story and the consequences of your circumcision. My talk and your words have been translated into several different languages, and I know this would please you. Your tale has touched many hearts and is making a difference and helping bring change, and so your life truly had meaning. I am so proud of you, my lovely boy, you truly were an extra-special young man.

I know you would approve of my wish to help young people, especially young men, understand the need to talk about their problems, no matter how personal. Perhaps if I can show the agony of those left behind after suicide, then I might just prevent even one person from attempting to end their life. They need to know that they will not be judged for admitting to having suicidal thoughts and that there is no shame in reaching out for help. I am so very sorry that I could not do this for you.

Since you died, I have been unable to listen to any of my favourite music, and Ste, Tom and James know instinctively to mute any gentle or evocative music, and I am grateful to them. It is only now, more than three years since you left us, that I am beginning to listen to music that speaks to me and transports me to our alone space, just you and me. My heart breaks anew when listening to Enya's "If I Could Be Where You Are" or my new favourite, a beautiful song by Imelda May, "11 Past the Hour". Although the lyrics make reference to "your sins", despite you having none, the otherwise apt words allow me to close my eyes and imagine me in your hugs that used to engulf me when we were together. The accompanying video touches my soul when I look up at the stars and speak to you. I cry for the dance we will never have at your wedding and for so much more...

For me, "11 Past The Hour" by Imelda May has become our song.

I know with certainty, my darling Lix – the name that only I used and which you touchingly signed off your last, loving words to me – that you would have been smiling down on James one Saturday soon after your death, when Ste arranged for him to be a team mascot at his favourite football club, Shrewsbury Town. I want you to know he had a memorable day meeting the players, having a pre-match kick-about and walking onto the pitch with his favourite player, Sean Whalley, of whom you heard James speak so often. Many photographs of your smiling little brother on that day still adorn his bedroom wall.

I also know that you would approve of my decision to share your savings between Tom and James, and that you would smile that I bought myself a beautiful heart-shaped locket, engraved with your last words to me. I wear it every day, close to my heart; you can guess whose photograph lies within. I have also bought a small, heart-shaped silver box in which I keep a lock of your hair. I cut only a small amount as you lay in your coffin in Canada and will never forget my longing to jump in beside you.

You perhaps already know this, but a few months after your death, I woke from a fitful sleep to see you clearly standing at the foot of the bed, smiling at me. This brought me much comfort, as you appeared happy, and I hope this is a sign that you are now at peace. I long for another such sighting, but there have been none. I can hear you saying, while grinning, "Mum, do you know how much effort that took to appear to you? Be grateful for that!" Of course, that would never be enough, but I do feel close to you always, especially when I am having my daily walk beside the sea, just you and me in my alone space. I cry, chat to you, ask where you are, and I hear your reply: "I'm here Mum, right beside you." I hear the words you would say to me, along with your witty responses to things that either happened in the past that amused you or new situations that I have experienced since you left us. It is the time I can most clearly hear your voice, and it is the time I can relive the memories I cherish. Sometimes, I am accompanied along my coastal walks by the seals that inhabit these shores, which you would love. I like to feel that you are the wind in my hair, the sun on my face.

James said something two years after your death that would have broken your heart. I had been asking him when he wanted me to put up the Christmas tree, as it was already the second week in December. He replied, "Not yet, Mum, it's still too early." I asked him if this was anything to do with your death, and he said, "Yes. I am not as bothered about Christmas. I am growing up, Mum, and now Alex is dead, it isn't the same." Of course, Christmas could never be the same for me again, but I naively hoped that for James, there would still be that childlike joy. Your adored little brother did not deserve to have his excitement over Christmas stolen from him. I have never felt anger towards you for taking your own life, Alex, just extreme sadness for your suffering. In that moment, I felt such deep sorrow that your desperate action impacted on the brother you loved so much. Tom largely keeps his grief to himself, and I know he has found peace in acceptance, but will always miss what can no longer be: you and him growing older, the bond of siblings, sharing life experiences and, as he has said, he will never get to have you as his best man when he marries. He, too, loved you as I know you did him. You would be so pleased to know that James is like you in many ways, and both of your brothers share some of your mannerisms. In coming to terms with your death, the bond between Tom and James has grown stronger, and I know this is what you would have wanted.

Of all that has happened since you died, this is the most surreal and memorable moment. It was the morning of the start of our trip to Canada, where we were to spread your ashes on your favourite mountain – an agonizing trip for us all. The last few pieces of luggage were in the hall waiting for Ste to load into the car. I had very deliberately not shown your brothers which bag contained your ashes. James, who at that age would never normally think to help, strode into the hallway, casually picked up the bag with your ashes from amongst several other items of luggage and placed it in the boot before climbing into the car. He was totally oblivious of the significance of this moment, but it was not lost on Ste and me. We both felt then, as we do now, that you would have chosen James to carry you out of your home for the very last time.

I have been unable thus far to look at the brief video footage I have of you, as it breaks my heart, but one day, when I feel strong enough, I will. If only I could have one more minute with you, one more lifetime, but I could never let you go. While I know that the sadness will never leave Tom, James and I, you will be pleased that your brothers are coping remarkably well. Tom is navigating his own journey through grief while working to conserve the natural, beautiful wilderness of New Zealand and making new memories and new friends. I know this is what you wanted for him, and you would be so proud of his resilience.

Do you remember when I arrived in Canada with a large supply of my homemade vanilla fudge that you and I loved? You left me in my hotel room for a few hours to sleep off my jet lag. When you returned, I asked you if you had tasted the fudge. "Oh yes," you replied with a sheepish grin. We laughed because I knew, so like me, you had over-indulged, and we then went on an extra-long walk to compensate. I also have precious memories of you and I enjoying ice cream, our favourite food. It couldn't be just any ice cream; it had to be homemade, organic or an extra-special gelato, and we always shared our favourite flavour, you know the one. The first few times I bought it after you died, I had to throw it away because I knew I would never again be able to share it with you. I can still hear you saying, as you often did, how you wished you had not inherited my sweet tooth.

I know that you encouraged me in your last letter to be happy again, which, as you knew well, would prove elusive for me following your death. It is impossibly hard to go on without you. There are times when it would be easier for me to disappear into the black hole of grief, but I know what you would say to me. How can I live with you being dead? If only you had told me, and with hindsight, your choice of language implied, alluded, hinted at something not being right in our last conversation, only days before your death. Those words will remain private, but I can close my eyes and still hear your voice in my ear. I never want to forget how you sounded.

I realize that I have a choice and spending my days waiting to die in the hope of being reunited with you is no way to live – as a mum, this is not a choice I could make anyway. I aim to honour you by healing, in whatever way I am capable, as you wanted this for me when you wrote in your final paragraph: "Do not mourn me eternally, but rather live a life of fulfilment." You got that wrong, Lix, as I will forever grieve for you.

As I had often sat in your flat in Canada, chatting to you on my many visits, I know exactly where you ended your life in the most peaceful way you knew. I believe your last thoughts were of me. You would smile at that, saying, "How presumptuous, Mum." I returned to your room with Ste to retrieve some of your belongings and was plagued by the thought of your final moments. I was there when you took your first breath and felt denied by not being there when you took your last. I even feel jealous of those parents who hold their child as they die, and I am aware how desperate that must be. I was across an ocean, and this has caused me immeasurable agony.

Since you left us, I feel like I am living on the outside of the world looking in at the normal life I once lived and where I felt I belonged. I wonder, is this how you felt in your last years as you battled to find a solution to your pain? To quote your insightful but tragic words of how you felt following your circumcision, I too now feel like this since you left me: "The consequences have cast a dark shadow on my life. I once lived in colour, but now I exist in monochrome."

During the past three and a half years since that dreadful night when the news of your death reached me, I have had my eyes opened to the most beautiful and the cruellest sides of human nature. From the pain of our close relative and a friend who disappeared from our lives to the kindness of strangers, my grief journey has been illuminating. I've experienced cruel abandonment by those who knew me and you, as well as surprising acts by thoughtful, kind people who did not know me, never met you and now never will. The stark contrast of some – compared with how you treated people with compassion, kindness and empathy – has been enlightening.

I still find it almost impossible to look at your belongings, both clothes and special things, which I keep in memory boxes in a spare room. Sometimes, when I am alone, I indulge myself, peek into these boxes and bury my face in your favourite sweatshirt, where the smell of you is still present. It's the one you wore when you last hugged me. I feel your closeness and am frightened that the scent of you will go. I close my eyes and press it against my face, hoping it will smell of you forever. The scent is getting fainter, though, and this hurts so badly. I breathe in deeply and feel you close to me. I weep – sometimes silent tears, other times howling for you, for none of this to be true.

I have experienced many emotions since that horrific night including regret, guilt, love and fear, but, above all, I feel an overwhelming sadness that you left us. I wish with all my heart that my love for you had been enough to save you. I failed to protect you, to keep you alive. That you are dead while I still live defies the natural order, and if I could swap places with you, I would without hesitation. My grief will never go away but will be always with me, for the rest of my life. The unbearable sorrow of going on without you is endless, and the intense pain inside me is as deep as all the oceans in the world. You now exist within my heart, no longer a physical presence, but forever such an important part of my life.

My darling Lix, yesterday as I walked along the seafront, my tears flowed at how much I will forever miss you. It was a beautiful, sunny day, the sky bright blue, and I found myself begging for another five minutes with you. I looked up at the sky as I said these words and saw it was full of white criss-cross clouds like kisses from you to me. I desperately needed a sign at that moment, and I like to think that you sent it to me.

As I was walking beside the sea this morning, thinking of you as I always do, an idea came to me. I hope that one day there could be a new law in your name, Alex's Law, making it a legal requirement for all surgeons to fully disclose the risks to a patient or to parents contemplating circumcision for their son. It would no longer suffice to suggest that it is a "routine procedure". Only then, as you also suggested, can an informed choice be made. Yes, I know, I am thinking big, who knows what's possible? I never expected to give an interview to the BBC that would remain on their online front page as one of the most-read pieces that week. I certainly would never have pictured myself giving a talk at a worldwide conference and have professors of medicine interested in your words detailing your experience of circumcision. I could never have imagined writing a book, either. I do know how much your suffering has touched people and is helping to bring about change.

I am yet unable to say I have a new appreciation for life, although I have discovered peace in nature. I see beauty in rainbows – the name of our new house – and have always found beauty in the mountains and sea, just as you did. I know I am lucky to be alive and just wish that you had felt this, too. Life is a gift, it is precious, and you were so intelligent, handsome, much loved and had such a promising future ahead with so much to give, and yet your circumcision ended all possibility of that for you. I remember during one of our last holidays together you discussed your hopes for a loving relationship in the future and your desire to have one child. My darling, you would have been an amazing dad, as you had learnt through bitter experience what it took for a father to cherish a child.

Our lives will now forever be divided into before and after. Nothing will ever be the same, but you will always be the first number in my phone book – A is for Alex. This will never change and is forever reserved for you. Your birthday will always have a heart written beside the date on my kitchen calendar each year, the most wonderful day of my life; the day I had longed for when you made me a mum. Your life was too brief, my darling, yet I could not have loved you more. You will live on in our memories, your handsome smile that your Canadian friends said could light up a room, your humour and sharp wit and great empathy and kindness to others, your intuition, intellect and flair for cooking, your gorgeous grin, or did I write that already? The list is as endless as my love for you.

I wish I could hug you one last time, look into your gorgeous green eyes and tell you again how much I loved you. But you did know this. I wish with all my heart that I had another chance to love you. Until then, I will carry you in my heart for the rest of my life, forever my wonderful son, always just 23 years old. You and I will forever have our connection, and nothing can destroy that, not even death. Being your mum was both a privilege and an honour. I will always have three sons, and when your brothers look to the world with compassion, kindness and bravery, you will be with them, forever a part of them.

To the world, my darling son, you are just another young male suicide, but to me, you are the world. I am going to have to let you go now, just a little, as this is the only way I can stay here. My wonderful, precious son, it will only be the blink of an eye, and I will be with you again. You had a beautiful soul, Lix, and I saw this from the earliest days of your childhood. You are at peace now. You belong to yourself. Find your wings and fly. Until we are reunited, I find solace in the words I can easily hear you saying to me: "I am here Mum, just love me, as I love you."

To quote your last words to me, my darling,

"Love Always and Forever,"

Mum xxx

Such a precious memory: our last hike together in Canada

ACKNOWLEDGEMENTS

A special thank you to those family members and friends who have supported me since Alex's death and most especially those who have remained with me since that first night when hell knocked on my door – you know who you are. You did not need to experience or understand the depths of my pain to simply be there. Thank you also to the new friends I have made in moving back to North Wales. I am forever grateful.

This book would not have been possible without the love and support I have received from Tom and Steve. Tom, your big brother would be immensely proud of your constant encouragement, which has given me the strength to face each new day. Together with James, the three of you have given me the reason to keep putting one foot in front of the other. It is my promise to you all that I will continue to do this until my natural time comes to be reunited with my darling Alex.

ABOUT CHERISH EDITIONS

Cherish Editions is a bespoke self-publishing service for authors of mental health, wellbeing and inspirational books.

As a division of Trigger Publishing, the UK's leading independent mental health and wellbeing publisher, we are experienced in creating and selling positive, responsible, important and inspirational books, which work to de-stigmatize the issues around mental health and improve the mental health and wellbeing of those who read our titles.

Founded by Adam Shaw, a mental health advocate, author and philanthropist, and leading psychologist Lauren Callaghan, Cherish Editions aims to publish books that provide advice, support and inspiration. We nurture our authors so that their stories can unfurl on the page, helping them to share their uplifting and moving stories.

Cherish Editions is unique in that a percentage of the profits from the sale of our books goes directly to leading mental health charity Shawmind, to deliver its vision to provide support for those experiencing mental ill health.

Find out more about Cherish Editions by visiting cherisheditions.com or by joining us on:
Twitter @cherisheditions
Facebook @cherisheditions
Instagram @cherisheditions

Cherish
EDITIONS

ABOUT SHAWMIND

A proportion of profits from the sale of all Trigger books go to their sister charity, Shawmind, also founded by Adam Shaw and Lauren Callaghan. The charity aims to ensure that everyone has access to mental health resources whenever they need them.

You can find out more about the work Shawmind do by visiting shawmind.org or joining them on:

Twitter @Shaw_Mind
Facebook @ShawmindUK
Instagram @Shaw_Mind